THE UNEXPECTED VISTA

JAMES S. TREFIL

THE UNEXPECTED VISTA

A Physicist's View of Nature

✦

COLLIER BOOKS

Macmillan Publishing Company

NEW YORK

Macmillan Publishing Company
866 Third Avenue, New York, N.Y. 10022
Collier Macmillan Canada, Inc.

This edition is published by arrangement with
Charles Scribner's Sons

Library of Congress Cataloging in Publication Data

Trefil, James S., 1938-
  The unexpected vista.

  Includes index.
  1. Physics—popular works. I. Title.

QC24.5.T73 1985   530   84-19920
ISBN 0-02-096780-2

10   9   8   7   6   5   4   3   2   1

First Collier Books Edition 1985

Printed in the United States of America

With a profound sense of gratitude I dedicate this book to the memory of my grandfathers
Tomaš Trefil, who built
Karel Mestek, who remembered

Contents

THE UNEXPECTED VISTA

Introduction

ONE OF THE GREAT REWARDS OF HIKING OR BACKPACKING IS TO follow a trail and, suddenly and without warning, top a hill or come to a break in the trees and see the panorama of the countryside laid out before you. The view of the distant waterfall or rolling hills is often remembered as the high point of the entire excursion.

Such experiences occur in intellectual life, too. The moment of the "Aha!"—which cartoonists usually render by showing a light bulb coming on above someone's head—is an analogous happening. So too is the unexpected discovery that two things seemingly unconnected with each other are in fact intimately related. But while every hiker on a given trail will see the same view, the intellectual vista has the property that each person who comes to it can see something entirely different.

For example, imagine a line of motorists at a traffic light.

Each of them is looking at the same thing, a rectangular yellow box with three colored lights in it. But it is possible, even likely, that each of them *sees* something very different from the others. Suppose that the first person in line is an electrical engineer. To him, the traffic light is just one appendage of a large computer-operated grid that regulates the movement of vehicles throughout the downtown area. If you pressed him to go on—to describe the far reaches of his view—he might start musing about the light as one example of control systems and eventually wind up talking about the best-designed control system of them all, the human brain.

The driver of the second car in line is the representative of a large manufacturing firm. He sees the traffic light as an item that is built in a factory and sold to the city. After thinking for a while, he might go on to talk about the vast interconnecting web of economic activity, from mining to maintenance work, that has to be in place before something like a traffic signal is possible. He might even end with some general speculations about human beings as tool-making animals.

In the third car is an attorney. To him the traffic light might symbolize the set of laws human beings have developed. The mechanical or economic aspect of the device would be much less important than the rules of conduct it symbolizes. After all, at any given moment there are thousands of cars being driven in a city, and almost every driver obeys the traffic signals. Behind this display of mass obedience, our attorney may see the vast structure of the modern legal system, from legislators to courts to police officers. If pressed, he might go on to speculate about those aspects of the human character that require such a system to allow large groups of people to live together in relative harmony.

Each of our motorists sees the traffic light as part of a large interconnected network. The simple apparatus is seen to be just one aspect of an important system that governs some aspect of our lives. In a sense, the traffic light is like an object in the foreground of some marvelous medieval landscape painting, a device the artist uses to induce us to look further and see the rich tapestry of nature and civilization that lies behind it. I will call each driver's view of the traffic light a vista, a term that carries with it the connotation of wide-ranging view.

So the traffic light teaches us several important lessons. It tells us that the breadth and scope of the vista really have very little to do with the object that starts us looking. Whether the traffic light is seen as just a self-contained mechanical device or as part of a much larger system is primarily a function of the individual looking at it, and, more importantly, with that individual's training and habits of thought.

The traffic light also teaches us that two individuals looking at the same thing need not see the same vista. It's almost as if two hikers reach the same point in a trail, from which one sees a waterfall while the other sees a shady forest. We can often get an entirely different view of the world just by talking to people whose backgrounds lead them to see vistas different from our own.

Like other professionals, scientists have their unique vistas. It would be a mistake, however, to assume that all scientists share a common view of things. I was frequently surprised during the several years I spent as part of an interdisciplinary team in cancer research by just how much the training of the other team members affected the way they looked at our work. To a biologist a cell is part of an evolving, growing, living system; to a physicist it is a "black box" that processes energy and produces an ordered system; to a statistician it is one more bit of data to put into a computer program. Clearly, there is no such thing as a single, monolithic "scientific" vista.

What I'd like to do in this book is to share with you some of the vistas seen by people trained in physics, the science that deals with the laws of matter and motion, and as such concerns itself primarily with the inanimate world. Although the growth of such fields as biophysics and medical physics has tended to blur the dividing line between the physical and life sciences, knowledge from such fields has not yet become widely disseminated within the physics community. Therefore, the traditional view, in which physics is confined to the study of nonliving systems, is still widely held.

Two aspects of the vistas seen by physicists are sufficiently unusual to deserve special mention. First, many aspects of the physicists' vistas are unexpected and surprising, and, second, the vistas often show a surprising degree of interconnectedness. Both these properties have to do with a single feature of the discipline: the tendency to regard wide ranges of phenomena as being governed by a few basic laws of nature.

By the end of the nineteenth century, physicists had produced successful explanations of the motion of material objects (a field called mechanics), the behavior of heat (thermodynamics), and the magnetic and electrical properties of matter. Each of these three areas was seen to be governed by a few general laws. Mechanics, for example, was seen to be nothing more than the working out of Newton's Three Laws of Motion. All effects of heat and temperature were subsumed under the Three Laws of Thermodynamics (two of which are discussed in chapters 1 and 8). Four relationships known as Maxwell's Equations (see chapter 12) governed electricity and magnetism. Thus, everything that happened in the material world could be said to be a special case of just ten general laws, all of which could, quite literally, be written on the back of an ordinary envelope.

A number of popular books have appeared during the past few years in which the claim is advanced that the twentieth century has led us away from this concept of natural law toward a more mystical (and less mechanistic) view of the universe. Nothing could be further from the truth! The laws of quantum mechanics are different from the other kinds of physical laws mentioned, but that is to be expected, because they deal with a different kind of object. An electron, after all, is not a baseball or a satellite. I'll go more deeply into one aspect of this question in chapter 4, but I mention it here to make the point that most working physicists would not buy a mystical view of nature.

Actually, in the spirit of classical physics, we can say that all that has happened in this century is that two new fields of study have been added to the classical roster: relativity (see chapter 2) and the study of the behavior of atomic and subatomic systems, the discipline called quantum mechanics. Relativity, which encompasses the behavior of objects moving near the speed of light as well as our best current theory of gravitation, follows from a single law, the so-called principle of relativity. And while there is some debate about the details of the fundamental laws of quantum mechanics, it is clear that they are few in number. Thus, it may be said that modern physics takes the view that the behavior of everything in the world, from the greatest star to the tiniest atom, is governed by no more than fifteen general principles or laws of nature.

This state of affairs has a profound effect on the physicist's vista. If all of the uncounted phenomena in the universe have to be related, ultimately, to only fifteen laws, then it follows that many of these phenomena, totally unrelated on the surface, must have common roots. Thus, as our viewpoint moves back from the surface phenomena to the distant reaches of our vista, we discover that many other vistas are converging to the same end point, so that beneath the surface we see a thickly woven web of interconnections.

This suggests another aspect of the physicist's vista—the unexpected conclusions to which one can be led. Because even the most commonplace event is ultimately related to the laws that govern the entire physical universe, one is often drawn, in thinking about that event, to questions of the deepest intellectual content. We may, for example, start by thinking about an ordinary oil slick and find ourselves, unexpectedly, contemplating the nature of the stuff we call matter. Alternatively, we may start by describing the floor of an eighteenth-century English townhouse and wind up thinking about the ultimate beginning of the universe some 15 billion years ago. We may start by looking at an ordinary kitchen refrigerator and end up at the other end of time, contemplating the final fate of the universe. In other cases the vistas won't be so long, but each example in this book will, I hope, convey the idea of a universe where events and objects are tied together in a web whose ultimate origins lie in the laws of nature. Perhaps then we can, like Einstein, marvel at the incomprehensible fact that the universe is comprehensible.

My motives in bringing the physicist's vistas to your attention are twofold. First, I believe that the realization that the infinite variety of things we see in the material world can be reduced to a handful of general laws represents one of the great achievements of the human intellect. It deserves to be explained, and even celebrated. Second, even though we live in an age when the activities of science are beginning to be presented in an understandable way to the general public (in contrast to the situation a decade ago), too much attention is focused on the new and spectacular. All too often such reporting focuses on new technologies and ignores completely the philosophical underpinnings of the disciplines that make the technologies possible. This robs general readers of a chance to share the richness of the scientist's world view, a view that would enhance their appreciation of modern science.

Before examining some particular vistas in detail, we must attend to some preliminary details. It will sometimes be convenient to express very large or very small numbers in "powers of ten" or "scientific" notation. The rules for this notation are as follows:

> Every number is expressed as a number between 1 and 10 multiplied by 10 raised to some power.
>
> If such a number is raised to a positive power, the decimal point is moved to the right as many spaces as the power of 10 indicates (thus, we write the number 8,000 as 8×10^3).
>
> If the power of 10 is negative, the decimal point is moved to the left (we write .002 as 2×10^{-3}).

In this notation some common numbers are

10^{-8} cm	the size of an atom
10^{-13} cm	the size of a nucleus
10^{10} years	the approximate age of the universe

The use of the terms *atom* and *molecule* in the text may be somewhat confusing at first glance. These terms will be used in the usual way, with *atom* referring to a single chemical element and *molecule* referring to a collection of atoms bound together. In general, when I wish to talk about the fundamental constituents of matter without reference to a specific material, I will use *atom* as a generic term. When the text refers to a specific material such as water (which exists only in molecular form), I will use the term *molecule*. If this distinction seems overly pedantic, you may regard the terms *atom* and *molecule* as interchangeable in what follows.

When the discussion turns to the structure of the atom, I will use the following terms without added introduction:

electron: a light, negatively charged particle that normally moves in orbits around the atomic nucleus

proton: a positively charged particle 1,836 times as heavy as the electron, normally found in the nucleus of the atom

neutron: a particle as heavy as the proton but without any electrical charge, also normally found in the nucleus of the atom

FINALLY, I would like to thank a number of people who have figured prominently in the development of this book. Charles Scribner, Jr., provided the idea that got it started and thereafter spent an inordinate amount of time going over the manuscript in its many transformations, making sure that in the end it all came out right. Mrs. Nancy Lane retained her customary good humor in preparing the manuscript and seeing it through to final form. Mrs. Judith Peatross did the illustrations, though encumbered with a new infant. Bob Moran cheerfully turned the Montana state library system upside down to find unusual reference books. Thanks to you all.

James S. Trefil
Charlottesville, Virginia

1

Buckets
of Energy

THERE IS NOTHING QUITE SO ENJOYABLE ON A WINTER'S EVENING as an open fire. The warmth from the flames seems to have a special kind of charm that isn't shared by a central heating system, even though a physicist will tell you that the two kinds of heat are identical. If you think about it for a while, you will recall that heat generated from burning wood or coal can be harnessed by machinery to lift weights or move a vehicle. And yet, when you hold a piece of wood or coal in your hand it doesn't move, nor is it hot to the touch. How can anything so inert produce all these effects?

This is by no means a simple question. Some of the best minds in the history of science have stumbled over the relation between heat and motion, and it wasn't until the latter part of the nineteenth century that the issue was finally resolved. The difficulty is that there is no obvious connection between a quantity of fuel, a flame, and the work that can be performed by using that flame. We know that those items are connected, and in modern life we use various fuels to produce heat and power even though we, as individuals, may not understand the underlying physical principles. When you flick a switch to turn on a light, for example, you are using the end product of a process in which water is heated to produce steam, steam is used to drive a turbine, the turbine is used to produce electricity, and the electricity is transported to your home. So the ways heat can be converted to useful work are of immense practical importance.

The basic problem that scientists encountered in putting their ideas about heat into some order is the one we've pointed out—the lack of an obvious connection between heat and the large-scale motion it can cause. Because of this, it was felt that heat must be associated with some sort of fluid that flowed into and out of bodies as they underwent temperature change. The fluid was dubbed caloric. Such common effects as the heating of two sticks when they are rubbed together were once explained in terms of the "caloric fluid" being broken off from its normal resting places in the solid and appearing as heat. According to this theory, the amount of dust produced by the rubbing and the amount of heat generated ought to be roughly proportional. More dust meant more caloric fluid had been shaken loose, and that, in turn, meant more heat.

The first experimental evidence against the caloric theory of heat was supplied in 1798 by Benjamin Thompson (later Count Rumford). Born in Massachusetts, he left America after the Revolution, primarily because he had actively supported the Tory cause. He became a soldier of fortune, a womanizer, and (to use a southernism) a general scalawag in Europe. He obtained his title from the Elector of Bavaria for service in the army, and his brush with the caloric theory came when he was supervising the manufacture of cannons. At that time, there was a good deal of boring done on cannon barrels to bring them to military specifications. This was done by turning the barrel around so that the inside, or bore, came into contact with a sharpened metal bit. As the barrel turned, bits of brass were shaved off and the barrel heated up. It seemed to Rumford that, contrary to what you'd expect from the caloric theory, the less there was in the way of cuttings or scrap brass, the hotter the barrels got. He traced this to the sharpness of the bit—the sharper the bit the more cuttings there were and the less heat was generated. A dull bit, on the other hand, seemed to heat the barrel up without doing much useful cutting. Furthermore, regardless of how many or how few cuttings were produced, it seemed that heat could be generated as long as power was supplied to turn the barrel. Rumford even went to the trouble of immersing the entire barrel-turning apparatus in a tub of water and showed that the water could be made to boil. He demonstrated conclusively, in other words, that mechanical motion could produce heat, just as the steam engine had shown that heat could produce mechanical motion. This fact should have immediately established a logical connection between heat and energy, but it was not until almost half a century later that this connection was finally accepted. In the interim, Rumford's work was treated with the sort of benign neglect that scientists reserve for uncomfortable but irrefutable results.

The man who finally proved the connection between heat and mechanical motion was an independently wealthy amateur scientist from Manchester, England, named James Prescott Joule. In May 1847, he published a notice in the *Manchester Courier* that he would give a lecture in the reading room of St. Anne's Church, entitled "Matter, Living Fire, and Heat." This may well be the most unusual setting ever used for the announcement of a major scientific discovery. Joule described a series of painstaking experimental studies showing that there is a very precise equivalence between heat and different kinds of energy. One such experiment is shown in Illustration 1. A large weight was lifted up and then allowed to fall, turning a paddle immersed in a tub of water as it did so. The temperature of the water was measured before and after the fall, and it was found that the temperature increased.

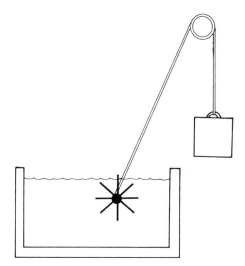

Illustration 1

Because the temperature increased, the process Joule used must actually have converted mechanical motion (the falling of the weight) into heat. Similar experiments with heating coils showed that the same effect could be produced using electricity, and Joule concluded that conventional forms of energy could be converted into heat, just as heat could be converted to energy of motion. When these experiments were accepted by the scientific community, the old caloric theory was at last laid to rest. It was now established that heat was a form of energy and not some sort of special fluid that permeated materials.

But what does this mean? When physicists use the term *energy,* they have a precise definition in mind—a definition that may or may not match the colloquial use of the term. When they say that something has energy, they mean it is capable of exerting a force over a distance. For example, the exploding gasoline-air mixture in a car's cylinder possesses energy because it can force the piston down and, ultimately, drive the car forward against the forces of road friction and wind resistance. When a force acts over a distance, we say that "work" is done, so that energy can be defined as the ability or capacity to do work.

In general, physicists in the nineteenth century recognized two broad categories of energy: energy associated with motion (kinetic energy) and energy associated with position (potential energy). A moving baseball is an example of an object possessing kinetic energy. When the baseball is caught it exerts a force on the catcher's mitt, a force that acts over a (small) distance to compress the padding in the mitt. Even if the ball hits something as unyielding as a concrete wall, there will be some deformation of the wall (and the ball) as forces are exerted. By virtue of its motion, then, the baseball can exert a force over a distance (do work), so it possesses energy according to our definition of that term.

Energy associated with position, or potential energy, can be illustrated by holding this book above the floor at arm's length. So long as the book is stationary, no work is done and no energy is being expended. But it is obvious that we could get the book to do work just by dropping it. The book has the potential for doing work, even if the work isn't being done right now. We say that it has potential energy.

The potential energy the book has, however, is dependent on its position. If it were on the floor, it would not be capable of doing work. On the other hand, our experience tells us that the higher the book is above the floor, the greater impact it will have when it hits and, therefore, the more work it is capable of doing—hence the more energy it has. Since it is gravity that supplies the motive power for the dropped book, we speak of gravitational potential energy.

If you think about Joule's experiment for a moment, you will realize that the raised weight possesses just this sort of energy, and that the potential energy of the weight is converted into the kinetic energy of the paddle as the weight falls. We can take this chain of reasoning one step further. At the start of the experiment, someone (or something) had to lift the weight up. This required exerting enough force to overcome the pull of gravity on the weight over the entire distance from the floor to its resting place. In other words, energy had to be expended in order to lift the weight up. This energy probably was supplied by the muscles of Joule's lab assistants, just as in a modern research lab it would be supplied by graduate students. It is this energy, then, that the weight expends as it falls, and which the rope transfers to the paddle blades.

This way of looking at things suggests a kind of balancing process in nature. In order to expend energy, a system must first acquire it, and the amount expended ought to equal the amount supplied. So long as we confine our attention to potential and kinetic energy, in fact, this will always be the case. Perhaps the best example of this sort of energy balance is the ordinary roller coaster. At the start of its ride, the energy, having been supplied by the lift motor, is purely potential. As the car starts down the track, some of this is converted to kinetic energy and the car speeds up, to the delight of the riders. At the bottom of the first incline the conversion is complete; all the original potential energy has been converted to kinetic energy. As the car starts to climb again, the reverse happens and kinetic energy is shifted back to potential energy. If there were no friction, this process could go on forever. The total energy of the system would remain unchanged, but the proportion in each of the two categories would constantly shift. Physicists refer to this sort of thing as a conservation law. No matter where the system is as time goes by, its total energy stays the same (i.e., it is conserved).

This tidy way of looking at the world, in which certain quantities are fixed and immutable, is very attractive. In fact, it is a measure of its attractiveness that the question of the nature of heat caused such anguish among scientists in the nineteenth century. Because if you think about the end of Joule's experiment, you realize that the original potential energy has disappeared (the weight, after all, is back on the floor), while at the same time the paddle and the water are stationary. It seems as if the energy has

simply vanished. The fact that the water is hotter than it was originally is interesting, of course, but if you allow only the sorts of
energy we have discussed so far in your balance, it is also irrelevant. It was Joule's great contribution to science to show that the
amount of heat generated is exactly what is needed to balance the
energy account. By this argument he was able to convince his colleagues that heat was nothing more than a third category into
which energy could be transformed.

With modern hindsight, this conclusion ought not to have
been surprising. We know that the water is made up of molecules.
If you imagine the paddle pushing itself through a collection of
such molecules, you realize that it will cause them to move faster.
Viewed on the atomic scale, then, the weight's potential energy
hasn't just disappeared; it has been used to increase the kinetic
energy of the water molecules. This increased molecular speed is
perceived as a raised temperature. What Joule's work showed was
that heat was not some sort of mysterious substance that could
destroy energy, but simply energy in a hitherto unrecognized form.
Subsequent work by Joule and others not only verified this statement, but showed that the amount of energy converted into heat
is always equal to the difference between the original and final
energies of the system.

So the appealing view of nature in which energy is always
conserved, and in which apparent changes are simply the conversion of energy from one form to another, is restored once we rec-
ognize heat as a special form of kinetic energy. We can summarize
this result in the following statement:

> Heat is a form of energy, and energy is always conserved.

This statement is known as the First Law of Thermodynamics.

There is a useful analogy that can help us understand this
principle. Imagine a series of buckets, each bearing a different
label. One might read "gravitational potential energy," another

"heat," another "kinetic energy," and so on. If you have a gallon of water, you can choose to put it all in one bucket, you can shift it from one bucket to another, or you can distribute it among the buckets. But no matter what you do, there will always be a gallon of water in the system. In an exactly analogous way, the total energy of any isolated system will always be the same, no matter how it is moved around among the different "buckets."

A very important lesson can be learned from the events that led up to the formulation of the First Law. Whenever we encounter a situation in which energy seems to be created or destroyed, our first concern should be to see if we haven't left out a bucket. Before Joule, the missing bucket was the one labeled "heat," and his contribution was to realize that if we included heat in our considerations the apparent imbalance could be eliminated.

Although Joule first put the conservation of energy on a firm experimental footing, Julius Robert von Mayer, a German physician working in Java, came to the same conclusion by a different route. He noted that the venous blood of his patients was a much brighter red in the tropics than it would have been back in Europe. He reasoned that this effect was due to the patient's body extracting less oxygen from the arterial blood because it needed to generate less heat in the tropics than it would have in colder climates to maintain normal body temperature. He concluded that body heat must be derived from energy stored in food, and thus came to the same conclusion on energy conservation that Joule demonstrated in his laboratories.

Now let's think once more about a wood fire. There is an apparent creation of energy: the piece of wood going into the fire possesses neither gravitational nor kinetic energy, and yet it produces heat. How can we square this with the First Law? If we take a clue from our historical precedent, our first attempt to resolve this dilemma should focus on the possibility that we are leaving some category of energy out of our considerations.

As was the case with heat, we can uncover this neglected type of energy by thinking on the microscopic level. We know that an

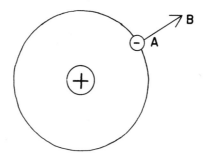

Illustration 2

atom has a structure like that in Illustration 2, in which negatively charged electrons circle around a positively charged nucleus. Since opposite electrical charges attract each other, we know that if we wanted to move an electron from the point labeled *A* to the point labeled *B*, we would have to apply a force over a distance—that is, do work. The electron at point *B* would then have acquired energy by virtue of its position, in much the same way that a book lifted from the floor to shoulder level has acquired gravitational potential energy. If the electron were to fall back to point *A*, the energy it had acquired would be converted to energy of motion, just as a falling object converts gravitational potential energy to the energy of motion. There is in fact a clear analogy between the energy an electron possesses by virtue of its position in the atom and the energy a massive object has by virtue of its height above the earth. Consequently, we can speak of "electrical potential energy" and add this new "bucket" to those we have already assembled.

A given atom or molecule will always have some electrical energy stored in its electrons by virtue of their position. This is sometimes called chemical potential energy. Wood, coal, and other fuels are no exception to this rule, although their molecules are often very complicated indeed. In the process of burning, these complex molecules combine with oxygen and break up into many smaller molecules (the most common being carbon dioxide). Each of these smaller molecules also has a certain amount of energy stored in its electrons by virtue of their position. So there are three energies involved in the analysis of the wood fire: the electrical potential energy stored in the original wood and oxygen molecules, the electrical potential energy stored in the final products of the burning, and the heat given off by the fire. Although the necessary arithmetic is a little complicated, it can be shown that the electrical potential energy after the burning is less than it was before. If we compare this energy deficit with the amount of heat produced by the fire, we find that they are equal. Burning, then, simply converts electrical potential energy to heat. Once again, we find that introducing a new energy category restores the conservation law that appeared to have been broken.

Burning is only one example of reactions in which electrical potential energy and heat are interchanged. There are others (such as those involved in cooking) in which the process occurs in the reverse direction. Heat energy is added to a system in order to initiate chemical reactions, and the stored electrical energy is greater after the reaction than it was before. But in all cases, the First Law holds true.

In the late nineteenth century there occurred a very interesting and little known controversy that hinged on the conservation of energy. The debate involved William Thomson (Baron Kelvin), who was responsible for converting Joule's careful experimental results into the mathematically rigorous and far-reaching statement of universal energy conservation. The subject of controversy was the process that allows the sun to radiate so much energy to its surroundings. It is relatively simple to find out how much energy the sun is producing. We know how much energy falls on the upper atmosphere of the earth—about 1.4 kilowatts per square meter. If you imagine a sphere whose radius is as large as the earth's orbit and whose center lies in the sun, you can see that this same amount of energy streams through every square meter of that sphere's surface. Furthermore, you know that the total energy emitted by the sun and total energy passing through the imaginary sphere have to be equal. Therefore, multiplying the area of the surface of the sphere in square meters by 1.4 kilowatts gives the total amount of energy emitted by the sun each second. As you might expect, the amount of energy radiated is astronomical, in both senses of the word.

Kelvin knew of only two sources from which the sun's energy could be derived: chemical reactions converting electrical energy to heat, and the gravitational potential of the sun. If the sun were slowly shrinking, then particles moving closer to the center would give up gravitational potential energy. Kelvin believed that this was the sun's energy source. From his calculations, he concluded that the First Law implied that the sun had been around only a very short time—about 100 million years or so. This statement, coming from the most famous physicist of the day, caused quite a stir at a time when geologists and evolutionists were saying that the age of the earth was measured in billions, not millions, of years. In order for Darwinian evolution to occur, long periods of time would have to pass while genetic changes accumulated to the point where the large variety of life we see could have developed. When Kelvin, using his calculations of the sun's energy sources, said, "I'll give you a hundred million years and no more," it seemed that a major conflict was brewing.

As it turned out, there was no conflict between the age of the sun as given by energy considerations and the age of the earth as given by geologists and biologists. Kelvin had simply fallen into the old trap of assuming that the sources of energy with which he was familiar were the only possible sources, that there were no more "buckets" to be added to our energy picture. In fact, with the promulgation of the theory of relativity by Albert Einstein early in the twentieth century, a very important addition was made to the energy-classification scheme we have developed. The famous equation $E = mc^2$ is so much a part of our folklore that it scarcely needs introduction. It tells us that in addition to energy associated with motion and position, there is energy associated with mass. If there is a process in nature by which the mass of a

Tokamak, a fusion test reactor, under construction at the Princeton Plasma Physics Laboratory. Photo courtesy of Princeton University.

system is less at the end than it was at the beginning, then that process produces energy. This is exactly analogous to burning, in which the difference in the electrical energy before and after oxidation appears as heat.

So mass becomes yet another bucket for energy. We note in passing that since the factor c^2 (the square of the speed of light) that appears in Einstein's formula is very large, only a small amount of mass needs to be converted in order to fill a very large energy bucket. Indeed, if a block of cement roughly the size of the chair on which you are now sitting could be completely converted into energy, it would supply all of the power used for all purposes in the United States in a year.

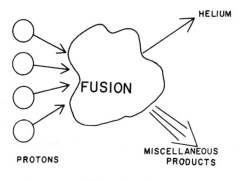

Illustration 3

Energy from the mass bucket keeps the sun shining. Illustration 3 is a simplified schematic diagram of the process. Four protons (the nuclei of four hydrogen atoms) come together to form a single helium nucleus plus some miscellaneous lightweight particles (the exact nature of these other particles needn't concern us here). We say that the hydrogen is converted into helium through nuclear *fusion*.

We can perform the same sort of analysis on the fusion process that we did for burning—add up the energies before and after and see if there is a deficit. In this case there is a rather sizeable one because the mass of the final helium nucleus, when added to the masses of the miscellaneous products, is less than the mass of the four original protons. This difference in mass is converted, according to Einstein's formula, into energy in its more conventional forms (primarily kinetic energy of particles). This is the energy we eventually see as sunlight.

In a sense, the fact that the sun still comes up and shines every day after billions of years is a proof of Einstein's theory. In addition, even though the sun converts about 600 *million* tons of hydrogen to helium each second, the sun is so huge that it will be many billions of years before its supply of nuclear fuel gives out. Thus, Kelvin was right in his assertion that the sun would eventually burn up all its fuel, and that this process would be governed by the First Law. He just didn't realize that another, infinitely more powerful source of energy was involved and waiting to be discovered.

So, at the present time we know of three types of energy—mass, kinetic, and potential—with several subclasses of the last two. In fact, physicists often ignore the distinctions we have been making and speak simply of mass-energy as one indivisible entity. Whether this represents the final word on the subject is, of course, a matter of speculation. Certainly the experience of the past century gives little support to those who would argue that there is no more to learn about energy. But it seems safe to say that whatever new buckets are uncovered in the future, the First Law, and the constancy in nature that it implies, will survive.

2

It All Depends
on Your Point of View

THE HISTORY OF SCIENCE HAS MANY EXAMPLES OF DEVELOP-ments that changed our view of man's place in the universe. Until the end of the Middle Ages, the accepted opinion was that the earth was at the center of everything and that all heavenly bodies (including the sun) circled around it. After Copernicus, we accepted the idea that the earth was only one of several planets circling the sun. Later it came to be realized that the sun itself was only one of many stars in the Milky Way galaxy. Today, we realize that the 10 billion stars in our galaxy are only one such collection, and that there are more than a billion other galaxies in the observable universe.

Of the discoveries listed in the previous paragraph, the one that has the most immediate effect on us is the first. The fact that we sit on a spinning globe means that every object on earth behaves a little differently from the way we might expect it to behave.

The first modern scientist to think about why this should be so was Gaspard Gustave de Coriolis. Coriolis was trained as an engineer in Paris in the early nineteenth century and spent a good part of his life teaching at the École Polytechnique, France's elite technical school. (He is remembered there as the man who ordered that water coolers be placed in the classrooms—coolers that the students still call Corios.) He was interested in designing machines, and, in particular, with finding out how much stress a machine frame would have to withstand because of the motion of its parts. This led him quite naturally to consider the effects of moving frameworks on the motion of fluids. In 1835 he published a paper in which he showed that because the earth rotates, the motion of fluids on its surface will be distorted. Instead of moving in a straight line, fluids will be deflected into the kind of swirling patterns you often see in satellite pictures of storms.

This result is at first very puzzling. Back in 1687, Isaac Newton had enunciated what has come to be regarded as one of the guiding principles of the physical world—the First Law of Motion. This law states that any object will remain in a uniform state of motion unless acted upon by a force. A particle moving in a straight line, for example, must continue to move in a straight line unless some outside agency intervenes to cause it to deviate. Conversely, if we see a particle deviating from straight-line motion, the First Law tells us that a force must have acted. But if the "particle" in question is a molecule of air in a hurricane wind, we know that it will move in a curved path even though there is no force around that appears capable of making it do so.

We can understand how this apparent dilemma is resolved by thinking about a simple situation. Suppose someone stands at the North Pole and throws a baseball to someone standing at the equator. If the earth were not rotating, the ball would follow a straight line between the two players, as shown in Illustration 4A. It would make no difference if we observed the ball's flight from the ground or from a spaceship parked above the earth. We would see the ball following a straight line in either case.

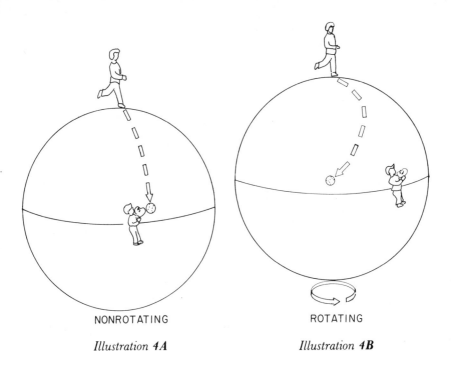

NONROTATING

ROTATING

Illustration 4A

Illustration 4B

But we know that the earth does rotate. In the real world, an observer in a spaceship would see a sequence of events like that shown in Illustration 4B. The ball would be thrown, and, since it would be unaffected by any force, it would travel in the Newtonian straight line. While the ball is in flight, however, the catcher standing at the equator would move along with the earth, and the net effect would be that the ball would fall behind him. This is a perfectly understandable situation, but to the catcher things look a little strange. He sees the ball thrown toward him from the pole. As it moves along its path, however, it begins to be deflected toward his left, ultimately falling to earth at the spot shown.

As far as the catcher is concerned, he is not moving. He is, after all, standing with his feet firmly planted on the solid ground. From his point of view, the deflection of the ball in flight can only be due to the existence of a force. So we have two different descriptions of the same event. The observer in the spaceship sees no forces acting on the ball, but the catcher does.

Which one is right?

If you think about it for a while, you'll realize that both observers are "right" in the sense that they each give a perfectly accurate description of the events they see. What they disagree about is the interpretation of these events. The observer in the spaceship sees a particle moving in a straight line in the absence of a force, while the catcher sees a particle being deflected by the presence of a force. In other words, an observer sitting in a rotating frame of reference (such as the earth) sees a force acting, while an observer standing outside the frame does not. Forces like this, whose existence depends on the point of view of the observer, are usually called apparent or fictitious forces by physicists. The force that causes the deflection of the moving ball is called the Coriolis force, after the man who first explained it.

Incidentally, you'll notice from Illustration 4B that when the catcher sees the ball deflected to his left, he sees it moving in a curved trajectory in a generally clockwise direction. Had the pitcher been standing at the South Pole, the situation would have been reversed (see Illustration 5). The catcher would then have

Illustration 5A   *Illustration 5B*

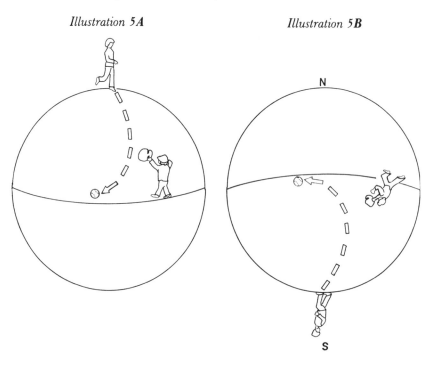

seen the ball deflected toward his right, a direction he would interpret as being counterclockwise. Thus, the rotation of the earth is ultimately responsible for the swirling pattern we see in the satellite photos. The wind moves in a straight line while the earth turns underneath it, and an observer on the earth sees the wind moving in a curved path in just the same way the catcher sees the ball moving in our example.

This explanation of the fictitious force associated with a rotating frame of reference is pretty much conventional wisdom in physics and can be applied to various problems. The patterns of the earth's ocean currents and prevailing winds are determined by the Coriolis force. On a more commonplace level, I can remember an ongoing debate among my fellow graduate students at Stanford as to whether or not toilets would flush differently in the Northern and Southern hemispheres because of Coriolis effects. Physics really does affect everything in life!

There is another way to look at this entire argument. Suppose we wanted to be truly perverse and insist that Newton's First Law be taken literally, and that we define a "straight line" as the path that will be followed by an object on which no forces act. If we did this, we'd have to conclude that whoever drew the meridians of longitude on the earth simply had gotten it wrong, for in point of fact a ball thrown from the North Pole will not move along one of these markings, as we have seen. The only case where a meridian and a "straight line" would coincide using this definition would be if the earth didn't rotate. To use a phrase familiar to science fiction buffs, we could say that the earth's rotation "warps the space" on the earth's surface, changing the map from that depicted in Illustration 6A to that depicted in Illustration 6B.

This approach, in essence, forces us to compare two different definitions of the common-sense term *straight line*. One of these, exemplified by the meridian of longitude, is geometrical in nature. We draw the line by dropping a perpendicular from the pole to the equator. The other is dynamical. We determine its location by observing the motion of a freely moving object. Our own everyday view is so earth centered, of course, that it's difficult for us to see

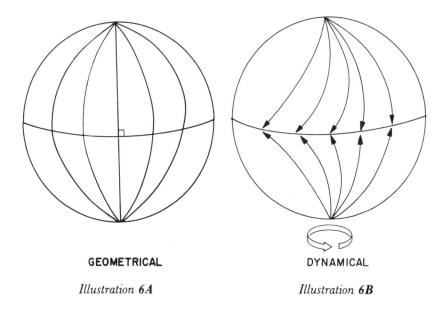

GEOMETRICAL   DYNAMICAL

Illustration 6A   *Illustration 6B*

the dynamic point of view as anything more than an exercise in academic hair-splitting, but there are many cases (as we shall soon see) where this intuitive certainty deserts us.

If we take the dynamical point of view seriously, this example shows us that there is an intimate connection between the point of view of the observer, the question of whether or not a force is acting, and the type of coordinate system that seems reasonable.

Albert Einstein was the first modern scientist to see the full implications of this point of view. If something as ordinary as the Coriolis force can depend on the point of view from which we observe events, what does this say about other phenomena we have taken for granted? What about gravity? Is it a true force, or does it, too, depend on the point of view of the observer?

One way of answering this question is to ask if there are any common experiences that seem to mimic the effects of gravity, experiences that make us seem heavier or lighter than we actually are. If you've ever ridden in an elevator, you know that the answer is yes. When the elevator starts to accelerate upward, you feel pulled down, heavier. When it slows down, you feel as if you're floating—lighter. If you were standing on a scale, these sensations would be registered—you'd get a higher reading when the elevator started, a lower one when it stopped. In other words, it appears that an acceleration or deceleration can produce effects precisely like those we normally associate with gravity. (The terms *acceleration* and *deceleration* are not usually distinguished in physics. An acceleration is defined to be any change in velocity, and by this definition a deceleration is simply a negative acceleration. We will use the term *acceleration* in this general sense throughout the book.)

We can even go one step further in making this analogy between the Coriolis force and gravity. Standing in an ascending elevator, you feel forces pushing you into the floor and weighing you down. These forces would not be seen by someone standing outside of the elevator, who would simply see the floor being pressed up against your feet. Therefore, the gravitylike force associated with acceleration must be another of the fictitious forces associated with the frame of reference of the observer, just as the Coriolis force is. And just as our normal earth-centered view led us to assume that an observer standing on the surface of the earth has the "right" view of things, the same prejudice makes us feel that the observer outside the elevator is giving the correct description of what happens when the scale reading starts to change.

But what if we imagine doing this experiment where there is no obviously "right" way to look at things? Imagine, if you will, a spaceship far from any star or planet, accelerating with respect to an observer. If a person in the accelerating ship throws a ball sideways, the observer in the other ship will see the floor of the accelerating ship move up and hit the ball. To the person who threw it, however, the ball simply fell in an arc to the floor. As far as that person is concerned, the ball was pulled toward the floor by a force, and that force is indistinguishable in its effects from the

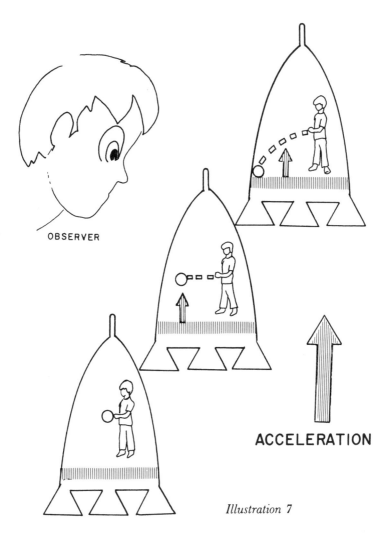

OBSERVER

ACCELERATION

Illustration 7

force of gravity that would exist at the surface of a planet. We cannot imagine an experiment that would allow the traveler to say that the "force" that causes the ball to fall is not gravity, but the result of the acceleration of the ship. If we asked the traveler in the spaceship to use the dynamical definition of a straight line that we have discussed, and then asked him to draw the straight lines along which a freely moving object would travel, he would produce a map like that shown in Illustration 8.

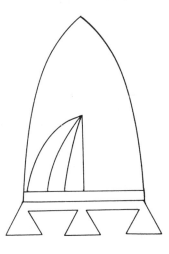

Illustration 8

Now the key point in this example is that gravity produced by massive bodies like the earth and the effects of acceleration cannot be distinguished from each other. In fact, it was precisely this sort of reasoning that led Einstein to the general theory of relativity in 1915. In essence, this is a theory of gravitation that puts forward, in precise mathematical language, the sort of argument we have given in the above examples. Because no observer can be sure that he or she is not accelerating, the central tenet of the theory is that every observer must find the same laws of physics to be operating in the universe, whether one is accelerating or is in a gravitational field. Or, to cast this principle in the terms we have been using, it should make no difference whether a particular effect is due to a fictitious or a real force; the outcome must be identical. Whether a force is fictitious or real becomes purely a problem of language: it is a totally irrelevant question as far as any physical effect is concerned.

We have seen this principle of relativity operating in our inquiry into the Coriolis force. Even though the catcher saw a force operating and the observer in the spaceship did not, both agreed that the ball would fall to the catcher's left. The same is true of the accelerating spaceship—both observers would agree as to where the ball ultimately fell, even though they disagreed as to whether or not a force was acting. That the laws of nature do not depend on the motion of the observer can be thought of as the central insight behind the relativistic revolution that Einstein started with his paper in 1905.

A short digression at this point on the historical development of relativity might be useful. There were, in fact, two distinct (but related) theories of relativity proposed by Einstein. What we are discussing here is the so-called general theory, based on the principle that *any* two observers, whether they are being accelerated with respect to each other or not, will see the same laws of physics operating in their frames of reference. This theory, as we shall see, is the basis for our modern understanding of gravitation. In 1905, a less comprehensive special theory of relativity was published. The special theory is based on the idea that two observers moving with respect to each other at constant velocity (i.e., not accelerating) will discover the same laws of nature. The special theory has many important applications, but does not apply to gravitation or the Coriolis effect. It is a special case of the general theory, the case of zero acceleration.

Let us now ask how our little thought exercise with spaceships leads us to a theory of gravity. The best way to make the analogy is to use the dynamical definition of a straight line and the idea of a "warped" space. We saw that the acceleration of the spaceship resulted in a warping of the space as seen by someone in the ship. If acceleration and gravity are to be truly equivalent, then it must be true that a collection of mass will produce exactly the same kind of warping that an acceleration would. A person standing on the earth, therefore, would have to find the same warping of space as would someone in an accelerating spaceship. Both would, in short, have to see a situation like that in Illustration 9.

If the person on earth threw a series of projectiles out to the side, they would follow exactly the same trajectories as they did in the accelerating spaceship. This is what is meant by the statement that it is impossible from any gravitational experiment for an observer to distinguish between standing on the earth or accelerating in a spaceship.

Illustration 9

We can carry this train of thought one step further. So far we have talked only about small-scale effects of gravity, such as its effect on falling bodies. But what about the large-scale effects, such as those connected with the orbits of the planets? A thought exercise can be used to show the connection between small- and large-scale phenomena. Imagine the observer in Illustration 9 throwing baseballs. Each would follow the usual parabolic path, as shown in Illustration 10, and the harder they were thrown the farther

Illustration 10

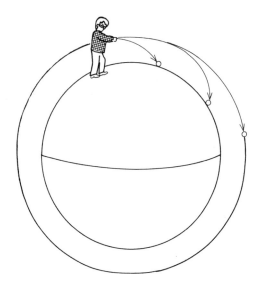

they would travel. You can imagine that if the ball were thrown at just the right speed, it would be able to travel all the way around the world, as shown. That ball would then be in orbit and would be a satellite of the earth, a small moon. It was reasoning like this that led Newton to suggest that gravity was responsible for the orbits of the planets.

According to this view of things, then, the kind of motion we normally associate with the force of gravity is not due to a force at all, but is simply the result of various objects moving along "straight" lines. The only difference from our normal way of looking at things is that in this view the "straight lines" are not straight in the geometrical sense, but are warped by the presence of matter. This point of view has one important advantage over the conventional outlook. There are no fictitious forces, because there are no forces at all. Everything we see is simply a result of the effects of matter on geometry.

It may seem at this point that all we have done is to take a rather strained interpretation of the effects of motion on observed events and put together a somewhat abstract way of looking at the world. As it happens, however, there are a few situations in which the relativistic viewpoint predicts different results than the conventional outcomes, so it is possible to see which of the two is right by conducting an experiment.

One of these experimental situations is easy to visualize, using the example of the accelerating spaceship (see Illustration 11). Suppose the person inside decides to shoot a beam of light across the ship from the point marked A on one wall. While the light is crossing the ship, the acceleration will move the opposite wall up so that the light strikes at the point B, below the level of A. To the person on the ship, it will appear that the light has "dropped" while in transit, just as a ball would in the presence of a gravitational force. The amount that the light would actually drop would be very small, of course, since light crosses the spaceship in quite a short time. Nevertheless, the effect could be measured with precise detectors. If we are to take seriously our parallel between acceleration and gravity, we would have to conclude that

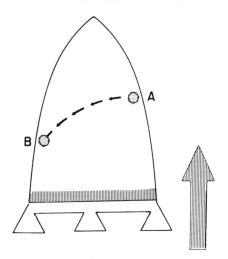

ACCELERATION

Illustration 11

relativity must predict that light will fall or be deflected when it comes near a massive object like the earth or the sun.

In point of fact, it was Arthur (later Sir Arthur) Eddington's confirmation of this prediction in 1919 that prompted the rapid acceptance of Einstein's theory of relativity by the scientific community. He took pictures of a star field before and during an eclipse of the sun and measured the apparent deflection of the position of a few stars (see Illustration 12). It was necessary to

Illustration 12

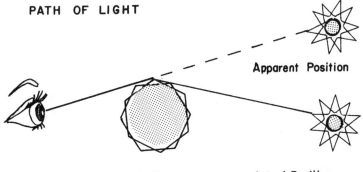

PATH OF LIGHT

Apparent Position

SUN   Actual Position

wait for an eclipse so that the stars near the sun would be visible and not lost in the normal solar brightness. When the measured deflection turned out to be the same as that predicted by Einstein (and different from that predicted by the usual theories), the geometrical viewpoint we have been developing was transformed from an academic abstraction into one of the central tenets of modern science. In the sixty-four years since that historical event, general relativity has met every experimental test to which it has been subjected. There is ample reason, therefore, to take it quite seriously as a view of the ultimate nature of gravitation.

It is a revolutionary way of looking at the world. The central idea is that there is no "correct" way of describing any set of events—all such descriptions are relative. Different observers may give very different descriptions of what they see, but they all must agree on the ultimate outcome of events and on the basic laws of nature that lead to those outcomes. Thus, the criterion for truth in physics shifts from what is reasonable from the point of view of some hypothetical "God's eye" observer to whether or not all observers will agree about a particular law, regardless of their relative states of motion. This is quite a change from the absolute space and time imagined by the followers of Newton in the eighteenth and nineteenth centuries.

It also differs from classical physics in the level of importance it attaches to geometry. Whereas in the conventional view of the world geometry simply provides a useful framework into which dynamical events fit, in this relativistic view the geometry itself is altered by the presence of matter and, in turn, determines the way matter will behave. With Einstein, geometry became a full partner in the physical world.

This may turn out to be very important indeed if new ideas about unified field theories come to fruition (see chapter 12). According to these theories, all forces in nature—the strong force (which holds the nucleus together), electricity and magnetism, the weak force (which governs radioactive decay), and gravity—are really different aspects of a single, unified interaction. We can speculate that if this is true, and if, as we have seen, gravity is not really a force at all but a manifestation of the interaction between matter and geometry, then *all* the forces in nature may ultimately be the same. It may be, in other words, that there are no forces at all, but only the deformations of space due to the presence of different kinds of matter.

This would be an interesting conclusion from a philosophical point of view, but, if relativity should really turn out to be the paradigm for the ultimate theory of matter, there is an even more interesting point to be made. All the great monuments of classical physics—the laws of mechanics, electricity and magnetism, and thermodynamics—are essentially summaries of experimental findings. The general procedure was to collect large numbers of facts and then bring them together into a coherent theory. With general relativity, however, this process was reversed. Einstein arrived at the theory without any reference to experiment. Instead, he conducted a sophisticated version of the kinds of thought experiments we've been talking about in this chapter. It was definitely a case of theory first, experiments later.

So, in a sense, if this is how the ultimate theory of matter comes about, it will mean we have come full circle. The Platonic ideal of knowledge gained through pure reason, so often maligned for its supposed evil effects on science, may bring us closer to the truth than we have imagined.

3

The Well-Balanced Universe

MANY YEARS AGO, WHEN I WAS A STUDENT AT OXFORD, I LIVED in a most peculiar house. The landlord claimed that because the house had been built in the seventeenth century, he was prevented by various ordinances from making any repairs. I never found out whether this was the truth or just an excuse, but the old place certainly sagged in a picturesque way. This point was brought home vividly one evening when a guest dropped a squash ball. It rolled erratically over the undulations in the floorboards and finally stopped while balanced precariously atop one of the higher elevations. From that point on, sending a ball on a roller coaster ride around the floor became a favorite way of relieving the seriousness of the endless bull sessions that are part of student life. Some of my colleagues became quite skillful at bringing the ball to rest at a designated hill or valley, and that spring we all got to know the topography of the floor pretty well. What we didn't realize was that the pastime we'd invented was an excellent demonstration of one of the most important processes in nature—the process by which systems come to, and stay in, equilibrium.

One of the most astonishing things about our universe is that it has existed more or less in its present form for so long. The earth, for example, has maintained its present distance from the sun for over 4 billion years, a fact that has been crucial in the development of life. The sun itself is a magnificent example of stability. It has poured out energy at roughly its present rate since its birth 5 billion years ago, and we can expect it to continue doing so until its death 5 billion years in the future.

On the other hand, unstable systems are also part of our everyday life. Sudden changes in the weather are evidence of the basic instability of the earth's atmosphere. This particular instability is very much on my mind as I write this, since several inches of unexpected snow is falling outside my window. Other natural disasters such as avalanches and floods (on the earthly side) and supernova (on the astronomical scale) are further examples of instabilities. The surprising thing is that all of these systems, stable and unstable, can be understood by analogy with the ball rolling around the floor in that old house. When the ball comes to rest, it may do so in one of the three situations in Illustration 13. In each

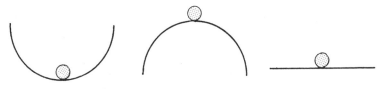

Illustration 13

case, we say that the ball is in equilibrium when the downward force of gravity on the ball is exactly balanced by the upward force exerted by the floor. Nevertheless, we can readily see that the three balancing acts are fundamentally different. The way to uncover this essential difference is to think about what happens when we move the ball a slight distance away from its equilibrium position.

If the ball is nestled in a valley, as on the left, then giving it a push will have little effect. As soon as the ball starts to roll up the sides of the valley, it will slow down, stop, and roll back toward its original position. Systems like this, in which small perturbations do not result in large changes, are said to be in stable equilibrium.

On the other hand, if the ball has come to rest on top of a hill, as in the center sketch, the situation is quite different. Giving the ball a small push in this case will start it downhill, and, once started, the ball will never come back to its original position. This is an example of unstable equilibrium in which a small perturbation leads to a large change in the system.

The intermediate state between stability and instability is seen in the situation shown on the right. In this case of neutral equilibrium, a small push leads to small changes in position and neither a return to the original position nor a runaway motion.

One particularly fruitful way to analyze this situation is to think of it in terms of energy. Anyone who has ever tried to move a piano up a flight of stairs knows that it takes a lot of energy to move something up and considerably less to move it down. The state in which the piano is upstairs, then, is of much higher potential energy than the state in which the piano is downstairs. In an exactly analogous way, the state in which the ball is at the top of the hill possesses a higher energy than the state in which it is somewhere down the slope. Conversely, the state in which it is at the bottom of a valley has a lower energy than the state in which it is somewhere up the valley wall. In this "language of energy," we say that an equilibrium will be stable if moving the system a small distance from equilibrium requires an increase in the energy of the system, while it will be unstable if doing so lowers the energy of the system.

This analysis of stability explains why unstable systems in nature do not last very long. We have spoken of moving systems from equilibrium in a rather general way; the implication has been that the small perturbations from equilibrium were brought about deliberately. If we think a little about the ball balanced on top of the hill, however, we realize that it may be toppled without anyone taking deliberate action. A gust of wind, the slamming of a door, or even someone going by in the hall could do the job. At the microscopic level, we know that the atoms making up the ball and the hill are constantly undergoing random motion, so that the ball is constantly dancing around. In other words, *every* system in nature is constantly being subjected to perturbations of one sort or another. If a system like the ball is in unstable equilibrium, then sooner or later even microscopic perturbations will grow to the point where they will start it rolling down the hill. Once it starts, it won't stop until it is safely nestled in some valley where its energy is much lower than that with which it started.

These two facts—systems that can move to states of lower energy are unstable, and such systems are continuously being subjected to small perturbations—lead us to a very important general conclusion:

> Every system in nature will evolve
> to the state of lowest possible energy.

This statement is almost trivial when we apply it to the problem of a ball rolling across an uneven floor, but applies equally to every system in the universe. In the example of the ball on the floor, the energy of the ball is of the type we have labeled gravitational potential energy (see chapter 1). The hills and valleys in the floor correspond directly to maxima and minima in the gravitational energy possessed by the ball. We know, however, that there are many kinds of nongravitational forms of energy. A free electron in a metal might have an energy that looks like Illustration 14, in which the "valleys" correspond to places where positive ions congregate. If an electron moves from point A to point B, it does not actually move downward. In moving from A to B, the electron moves horizontally into a region of lower energy; it "rolls down

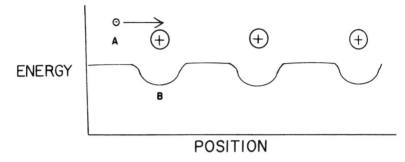

ENERGY

POSITION

Illustration 14

the hill" in a figurative sense only. The hollows are fluctuations in energy and do not correspond to any up-and-down motion of the electron. But to a physicist there is no essential difference between the shape of a floor and the shape of the curve shown in Illustration 14. Both are what the physicist calls potential surfaces, and the principle of lowest energy dictates that the system will wind up in a "valley," whether that valley is below the hill in a literal sense or not. All that is necessary is that the valley be at a lower energy than the hill.

To make the nature of this principle apparent, let's consider a third example. A drop of water falling through space could, in principle, take on any shape. Three possible shapes are shown in Illustration 15, ranging from a "cigar" to a "pancake," with a sphere as the intermediate configuration. The ratio of the two axes labeled *a* and *b* is a measure of how much the drop deviates from

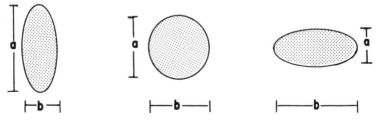

Illustration 15

a perfect sphere. If a/b is greater than 1, the drop is cigar shaped; if it's less than 1 the drop is like a pancake; and if a/b is exactly 1 (i.e., if the two axes are equal) we have a sphere. If we plot the energy stored in the drop as a function of a/b, we get a potential surface like that in Illustration 16.

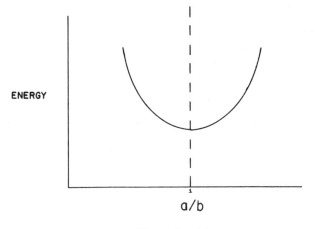

ENERGY

a/b

Illustration 16

The "valley" occurs when $a/b = 1$, from which we conclude that a drop falling in a vacuum will eventually form a perfect sphere. The reason is that the sphere, being the geometrical figure with the smallest area for a given mass of water, is the shape in which the least amount of energy has to go into creating a surface. One practical outcome of this result is a NASA program to investigate the possibility of manufacturing perfectly spherical ball bearings in space, where drops of molten metal can be allowed to fall free of the influences of gravity and air resistance.

More generally, the importance of this example lies in showing that, just as "hills and valleys" need not be taken in a literal sense in applying the energy principle, so "perturbation" need not refer to a movement in space. In the example of the ball rolling on the floor, we spoke of perturbations in terms of small displacements of the position of the ball in a hill or a valley, but we need not restrict ourselves to this definition. With water drops, the perturbation has to do with the deformation of the surface, not with the drop's position. This is a generalized sort of perturbation, defined in terms of deviations from the equilibrium situation. Clearly, such a definition has to be given to fit the particular problem being studied. As was the case with the ball on the floor, however, every system is always being subjected to minute generalized perturbations: the principle of lowest energy always operates.

Nature presents so many examples of this principle that it is difficult to single out a few for closer examination. The two I'm going to discuss are chosen because between them they illustrate the diversity of phenomena encompassed by the principle.

Consider a layer of fluid, such as water being heated from below in an open pan. After a while, we could expect to see a situation like that in Illustration 17: the layer of water near the bottom will be warm, and as we move up through the liquid the temperature will drop, leaving the coldest layer on top. Since water becomes less dense when it is heated, a given volume of water at the bottom of the pan will weigh less than the same volume of water near the top.

The situation we have just described is in equilibrium, but it's easy to see that it must be unstable. The total energy of the system could be lowered by interchanging equal volumes of hot and cold water, as shown in Illustration 18. Consequently, we

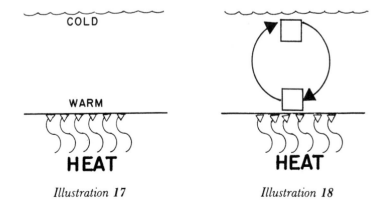

Illustration 17   Illustration 18

expect that the system will "roll downhill" from the situation shown in Illustration 17, where the water is stationary, to the situation shown in Illustration 18, where there is a constant transfer of warm water from the bottom to the top, accompanied by the corresponding transfer of cool water from the top to the bottom.

The mechanism by which such a transfer could get started (the perturbation, if you will) is easy to understand. Imagine a small volume of warm water near the bottom of the pan (see Illustration 19). Suppose that one of the small, ever-present perturba-

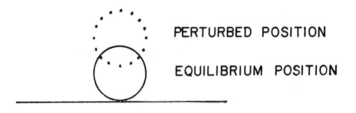

PERTURBED POSITION

EQUILIBRIUM POSITION

Illustration 19

tions caused this volume of water to rise slightly in the pan. In its new position it will find itself surrounded by cooler, denser water. Like a block of wood immersed in water, it will be pushed upward by ordinary buoyant forces, and this upward motion will occur before the heated water has a chance to cool off. As a result, the warm water will be pushed still higher and will find itself surrounded by still cooler, denser water. This, in turn, will lead to an increased buoyant force and a further upward movement of the warm water. Clearly, the net result of the small perturbation at the bottom will be to send a small volume of warm water to the top. An analogous argument can be made to explain the corresponding descent of the cooler water.

Once this interchange has taken place, the warm water that has risen to the top will radiate and cool off, while the cool water at the bottom will be warmed. We can expect a continuous motion of the water due to the instability we have discovered. We expect that the motion of the water will be as in Illustration 20, with warm water rising continuously in one place and cool water

CONVECTION
CELL

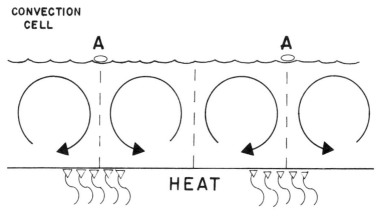

Illustration 20

descending continuously in another. This particular configuration is known as a convection cell. The energy principle is operating continuously in this system, for no sooner has a particular quantity of warm water from the bottom risen to the top than it starts cooling off, losing heat to cooler surroundings and sinking to the bottom. Normally, a heated fluid will have many such cells side by side, forming a continuous pattern. Next time you are boiling eggs, notice the spots where the scum collects on the surface of the water. Little bits of debris are carried along the surface by the currents to spots like those marked *A* in Illustration 20. At these points the cool water descends and the debris it has been carrying is trapped. Eventually, enough collects for you to see it when you look at the pan.

Convection cells will appear whenever a liquid or a gas is heated unevenly. For example, the atmosphere of the earth is heated much more at the equator than at the poles. If the earth didn't rotate, we'd expect a convection cell of the type shown in Illustration 21 to arise, carrying heat from the tropics to the poles.

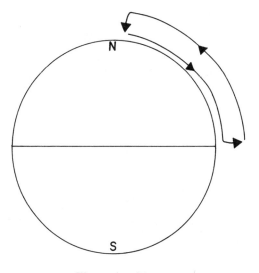

Illustration 21

Because of the earth's rotation (and the Coriolis forces discussed in chapter 2), the actual situation isn't quite so simple, but this general poleward flow of heat is what provides the power for the prevailing wind patterns on earth and is therefore responsible for much of the weather we experience. The same effect, operating in water, drives the Gulf Stream and the other great ocean currents.

On a smaller scale, heat stored in the brick and concrete of large cities warms the air above the ground, creating small convection cells. In this sense, cities create their own weather. This effect has been observed near suburban shopping centers, where the acres of asphalt parking lots serve as a heat source for columns of warm, upward-rising air. Even the drift of the continents is thought to be powered by convective effects having to do with the heat at the earth's core.

In these examples we encounter the kind of intellectual beauty that is at the core of physics. To see the essential oneness of a boiling pan of water and the slow drift of the continents, to understand that despite apparent differences the same mechanism is at work everywhere around us, is the ultimate reward of scientific training. The feeling of exhilaration that comes with such insights keeps men and women going during the years of study and frustrating research that make up most of the working life of the average scientist.

This point was brought home to me quite vividly a while ago when, in an article by the American physicist Frank Wilczek (*Scientific American,* Dec. 1980), I encountered one of the most intriguing applications I've ever seen of the lowest-energy principle. It has to do with speculation about the early history of our universe. It is now generally accepted that our universe started with a Big Bang—an explosion—immediately before which all matter was packed into a single, incredibly dense point. The expansion started about 10 or 15 billion years ago, and it is still going on today, with galaxies moving farther and farther apart all the time. In much the same way we traced the path of a ball on the floor, it is possible to speculate about the first instant of the Big Bang and to trace the history of the universe from its initial state to the present.

If we go back, not to the first minutes or even seconds, but to 10^{-35} seconds after the Big Bang (that's a decimal point and thirty-six zeroes before the first digit), the temperature would be so high that all matter would behave in the same way, regardless of its electrical charge or mass, and all the forces between particles would be the same. A physicist would say that this situation represented a high degree of symmetry. As the expansion of the universe progressed, the fireball produced by the explosion cooled off and distinctions between particles and forces began to become important. The symmetry began to disappear.

Perhaps the best analogy to this process would be the freezing of water. In the liquid state, water is highly symmetrical. If you were suspended in the ocean, you would see liquid water no matter which direction you looked. A physicist would say that this represents a state of high symmetry, since what you observe does not depend on the direction in which you look. If the water were to freeze, however, the situation would change. Ice crystals or snowflakes are hexagonal in shape, and hence frozen water no longer has the same degree of symmetry as liquid water—it does make a difference which way you look into a block of ice. Of course, we usually think of an ice crystal or a snowflake as symmetrical, because if you rotate either of them through an angle of 60 degrees, you have a figure that cannot be distinguished from the one with which you started. But this is not as symmetrical as liquid water, where a rotation through *any* angle will show the same aspect.

In just the same way, we can think of the universe as undergoing a series of "freezings" during which symmetries vanished. For example, at one stage in the early universe, the temperature was so high that the strong force (which holds the nuclei of atoms together), the weak force (which governs radioactive decay), and the electrical force were indistinguishable from each other. This situation has a high degree of symmetry. The temperature fell as the universe expanded, however, and something akin to "freezing" occurred. After the freezing, the strong force was distinguishable from the other two. Later on, another "freezing" separated the weak and the electrical forces, leaving us with our present universe, in which the three forces are very different from each other—a situation with a low level of symmetry. The exact order of these "freezings," as well as the time at which they occurred, are a subject of debate, but they were all finished well before the universe was one second old.

When water freezes, the energy of the ice is lower than that of the water that preceded it. We know this because we have to add energy in the form of heat to an ice cube to get it to melt back into water. In just the same way, the total energy of the universe after each "freezing" was lower than it was before. In a sense, then, the early evolution of the universe is just like a ball rolling down a hill, one more example of a system seeking its lowest energy state. But even this is not the end for us. Even assuming that we can trace the history of the universe back to the beginning by using the same reasoning we used for other systems, there is a far older and deeper problem facing us—the problem of what the universe was like before the Big Bang.

Some scientists simply refuse to consider this question, pointing out that it is not, properly speaking, a question that can be answered with the techniques of science. Others postulate that the present expansion of the universe will someday reverse itself, and that the subsequent contraction will once again produce the infinitely dense state that will serve as the beginning of a new Big Bang. To these scientists, the universe is a never-ending cycle of expansion and contraction, so the question of what was there before the universe is meaningless. For them there never was a "before." Both of these positions are intellectually defensible, and I have often used them when asked difficult questions by my students. But although both answers are logically consistent, I have always found them to be somewhat unsatisfying.

But now we have a new way of approaching this question. If we think about what must have existed before the beginning of our present universe, the best candidate is nothing—the vacuum. Why the universe exists, then, comes down to the question of why matter in its present form should have come into existence out of the primordial vacuum. And this, we now realize, comes down to the question of whether the universe with matter in it has a lower energy state than the universe without matter. If it is, then the vacuum would be, in a very real sense, unstable, and the appearance of matter, which began the Big Bang, would be just one more example of a system seeking the lowest energy available to it.

Of course, there's a big difference between being able to talk about an idea like this and being able to calculate the energies involved. At the present time the whole scheme is just an idea that hasn't yet been worked out. Nevertheless, it is an indication of the unity of scientific knowledge that the same principle behind a ball rolling on a floor may also account for the existence of the ball, the floor, and all the matter in the universe.

4

The Oil Slick
and the Electron

WHEN YOU PULL INTO A GAS STATION ON A HOT SUMMER AFTER-noon, you notice that the ubiquitous oil smears on the pavement seem to shimmer in the sunlight, taking on (at least momentarily) the colors of a peacock. Return on a gloomy day, though, and they are revealed to be nothing more than dirty black grease spots. A soap bubble may appear to have iridescent rings in it, even though the film is transparent. Spills of detergent in streams likewise take on colors, even though the detergent itself is white or colorless. Clearly this widespread phenomenon must tell us something about the nature of the quality we call color.

Thinking about this phenomenon will not only tell us about color, but about the nature of light itself. It is one of a large class of physical effects that operate by a principle known as interfer-ence. And although it may not seem obvious now, the colors on the oil slick are intimately related to such other common experi-

51

ences as the change in pitch in a trombone note when the slide is run out or the behavior of tidal waves following an earthquake at sea.

What all these disparate phenomena have in common is that they involve waves. The simplest way to visualize any kind of wave is to think of disturbances on the surface of a smooth pond. The wave in Illustration 22 is typical in that it can be characterized by three numbers: the distance between crests, which we call

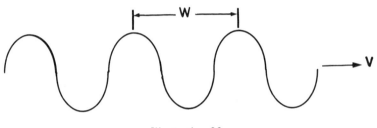

Illustration 22

the wavelength and denote by the letter W, the number of crests that pass a given point each second, which we call the frequency and denote by the letter F, and the speed with which the crests move along, which we call the velocity and denote by the letter V. Surf at a beach, for example, may have $W = 10$ feet, $F = 6$ crests per minute, and $V = 60$ feet per minute. It should be obvious from the definitions that if we multiply the distance between crests by the number of crests that pass in a given interval of time, we should have the velocity of the wave. In symbols, this means that $V = W \times F$.

In the oil slick problem, the most important property of waves concerns what happens when two different waves come together. Such a situation might arise if you threw two rocks into a pond. From each rock a circular wave would move out, and where the two spreading circles touched you would have two waves coming together at one point. What happens at that point

depends on how the waves arrive. If they arrive as shown on the
left in Illustration 23, with the crest of one wave showing up at

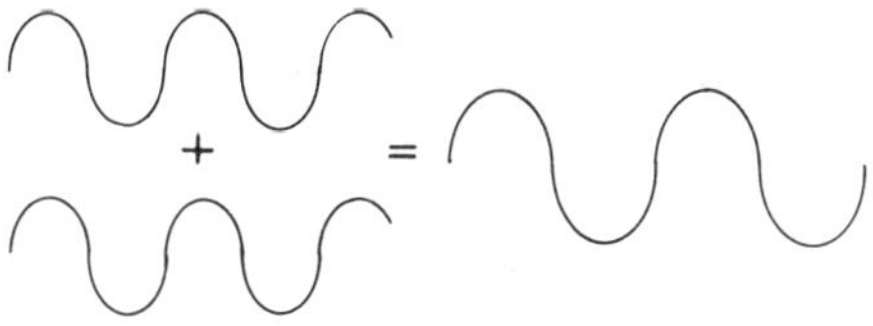

Illustration 23 (left) 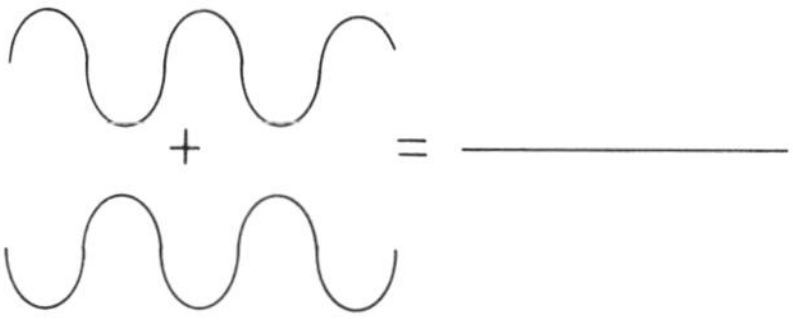   *Illustration 23* (right)

the same time as the crest of the other, then the two waves combine
to form a single wave twice as high as either of the two original
ones. This is called constructive interference. If, on the other hand,
they arrive as shown on the right of illustration 23, with the crest
of one arriving at the same time as the trough of another, the two
cancel each other out and the net effect is that the water will be
undisturbed at that point. This is called destructive interference.
Next time you're around a large harbor on a windy day, look at
the way the anchored boats move. There are many waves present
in such an enclosure, since the initial incoming surf reflects from
the docks and breakwaters. Some boats, located at points where
there is constructive interference, will be tossed around violently,
while others, located at points of destruction interference, will
move very little.

The existence of destructive interference is a unique feature
of waves. If two baseballs or two bullets come together in midair,
you can never get a result that corresponds to the total absence of
matter. You will always have two baseballs or bullets (or the
pieces) left after the collision. Not so with waves. If the conditions
are right, you can have two waves come together at a point, and
the net result would be the total absence of any wave. This is
important, because it means we can always tell whether a given
entity is a wave by seeing if it exhibits interference.

Take sunlight on an oil slick, for example. The presence of

iridescence can be construed as evidence that light is a wave not so very different from waves on a smooth pond, because the iridescence is actually a result of two waves coming together at your eye. These two waves are shown in Illustration 24. One wave corresponds to direct reflection of the sunlight from the surface of the

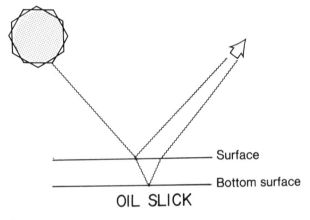

Surface

Bottom surface

OIL SLICK

Illustration 24

oil slick. The other corresponds to sunlight going into the oil, reflecting off the bottom surface, and emerging into air again. The oil slick, then, acts something like a plate-glass window. People on the outside can see their reflections, which means that some light bounces off the window, but people on the inside can see out, which means that some light goes through. The two waves (one reflected directly, the other going into the oil) start out with their crests and troughs aligned. Because the second wave has to travel a longer distance than the first, however, by the time the two arrive at your eye they are no longer aligned. The second wave will have slipped back with respect to the first, and crests that were initially aligned will not arrive together. Thus, in general, we would expect that complete or partial destructive interference would occur, and we would see either the absence of a wave (blackness) or only very faint light.

The only case in which this wouldn't be true would be if the

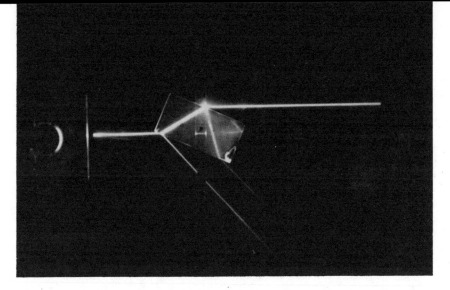

Light entering a block of glass from the left is partly reflected, partly transmitted, at the upper surface. The subsequent paths of the two parts of the beam can easily be seen. Photo by Judith Peatross.

extra distance the second wave had to travel was exactly equal to an integral number of wavelengths. In this case, the second wave would slip back just enough so that we would have a situation like that in Illustration 25.

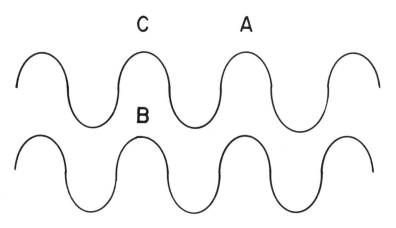

Illustration 25

Crest *B* on the bottom wave, initially lined up with crest *A* on the top wave, has, by the time both waves reach the eye, slipped back so that it is now aligned with crest *C*. Comparing this figure to Illustration 23 depicting constructive interference, we see that they are identical. We would expect, therefore, that whenever the difference in the distance that the two waves travel is equal to one or more wavelengths, we will have constructive interference and, therefore, we will see a bright light. (This is a slight oversimplification in that it ignores certain effects that are actually present, such as phase shift on reflection and the difference between optical and geometrical path lengths, but it makes the point.)

We can now begin our analysis of the oil slick by imagining the situation shown in Illustration 26, in which light of a single color strikes the slick at an angle. If we look at the slick from eye

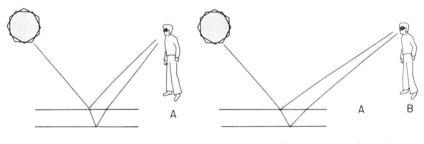

Illustration 26 (left)   *Illustration 26* (right)

level at point *A*, as shown on the left of Illustration 26, two waves that interfere at the eye are indicated (the fact that the waves are not precisely parallel has no effect on any conclusions we draw). In general, the difference in the distance that the waves travel will result in partial or total destructive interference, and little light will come to the eye. The person at *A* will not see a color on the surface of the oil slick. On the other hand, there will be some position, such as the one labeled *B* on the right in Illustration 26, in which the difference in the paths of the two waves will be just enough for the two waves to interfere constructively. In this case, the observer will see a band of color on the oil slick.

In fact, we can take this analysis one step further by asking what one would see if one simply stood near the oil slick and let one's eyes range over it, as shown in Illustration 27. In this case,

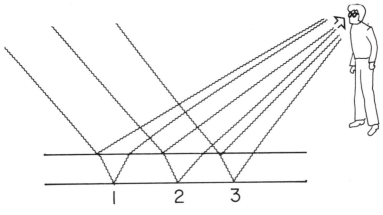

Illustration 27

there would be certain points on the oil slick where the conditions for constructive interference would be met. At these points, labeled *1*, *2*, and *3*, the second wave has slipped back one, two, and three full wavelengths, respectively, with respect to the wave that is reflected from the top of the slick. In this case one would see a band of color if one looked at the point labeled *1*, no color if one looked between *1* and *2*, a band of color at *2*, and so forth. In other words, the slick would appear to be an ordinary dirty brown except for several bands of bright color, such bands corresponding to those positions on the slick where the distance to one's eye and the angles involved are just right for constructive interference to occur.

An oil slick in the sunlight is not exposed to a single color of light, of course, but to a mixture of all colors in the visible spectrum. The quality that we perceive as color actually corresponds to the wavelength of the light that strikes our eye. Red light has a longer wavelength than violet light, with other colors falling between these two. The consequence of this fact for the appearance of the oil slick is easy to deduce. Suppose we are standing and looking at an oil slick being illuminated by sunlight, as shown in Illustration 28. If we look at a specific point, such as the one

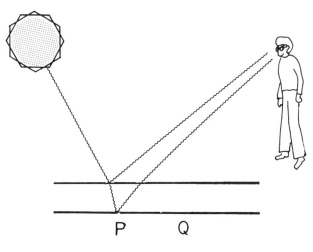

Illustration 28

labeled *P*, then the waves that travel the two paths shown will interfere at the position of our eyes. For most colors (i.e., for most wavelengths of light) the difference in path will produce partial interference. Consequently, these colors will not appear in the slick. There will, however, be one value of the wavelength (one color) for which this path difference is precisely what is needed for constructive interference. If we assume for the sake of argument that at *P* constructive interference occurs for the wavelength associated with green light, then when we look at point *P* on the oil slick we'll see a green band. This color arises because sunlight contains green light and the conditions for constructive interference are met for green at point *P*.

In a similar way, if we look at the neighboring point labeled *Q* in Illustration 28, the condition for constructive interference will no longer be met for green light, but it will be met for some other color, such as blue. Consequently, when we look at the slick we will see a series of colored bands ranging (in principle) through the entire visible spectrum. This is the familiar peacocklike iridescence.

From what we see when we drive into a gas station, we can therefore conclude two important things about the nature of light. First, it is a wave, and second, the different colors correspond to different wavelengths of the wave.

But waves in what? It is easy to picture a wave on water, since we've all seen them on oceans or lakes. It's also easy to think about something as common as a sound wave, where the crests correspond to regions where air molecules are more tightly packed together than normal. But it's hard to form the same mental picture for light, since we know that it can travel unaffected through vast distances of empty space. Exactly what is "waving" between ourselves and the sun when we see sunshine?

It used to be thought that space was filled with an invisible, intangible substance called ether and that light was a wave in ether in much the same sense that surf is a wave in water. This idea goes back to the Greeks, who assumed that the space between earth and the celestial spheres had to be filled with *something,* and the concept survived well into the nineteenth century. Ironically, it was an experiment using the interference property of light that showed there is no such thing as a universal ether of the kind assumed by scientists.

The experiment was done by two physicists, A. A. Michelson and E. W. Morley, at Case Institute of Technology (now part of Case Western Reserve University) in Cleveland between the years 1881 and 1887. The basic reasoning behind the experiment was this: If there is indeed all-pervading ether, then the earth, by virtue of its motion, must constantly be in the presence of an ether wind. This effect is similar to the breeze felt by occupants of a car moving through still air. The purpose of the experiment was to detect this ether wind by observing its effect on light.

Basically, the setup was like the one in Illustration 29. Light

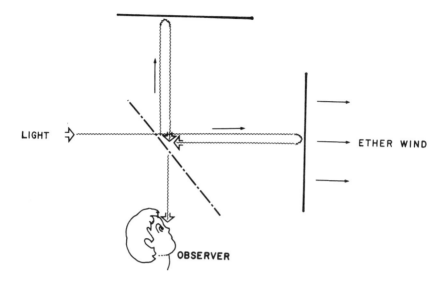

LIGHT

ETHER WIND

OBSERVER

Illustration 29

entering from the left first encounters a partially silvered mirror that splits the beam, much as the surface of the oil slick split the beam of sunlight in the previous example. The two parts of the beam then travel to mirrors at right angles to each other, are reflected, and return to a point where they can interfere with each other. If the ether wind is in the direction shown, blowing from left to right, then the time it takes the two parts of the wave to complete their respective journeys will be different, and some sort of detectable interference pattern will emerge. (The best way to visualize this experiment is to imagine starting two boats in a swiftly flowing river. One boat is to travel downstream with the current and then return against the current. The other is to cross the stream and return at right angles to the current. Clearly, if the two boats start at the same time and move at the same speed as they would in still water—for example, by having their motors running at the same speed—they will not return at the same time.)

For various reasons this experiment is usually done by orienting the mirrors one way with regard to the supposed ether

A. A. Michelson (1852–1931) performed an experiment with E. W. Morley between 1881 and 1887 which showed that there is no such thing as a universal ether of the kind assumed by scientists. Photo courtesy of the American Institute of Physics, Niels Bohr Library.

wind, taking measurements, and then repeating the entire process with the apparatus turned 90 degrees, so that no matter which way the ether wind is blowing its effect will be seen. But this sort of detail is not essential, since no matter how the experiment is done no ether wind is detected. Even with modern laser instrumentation this old result was held up, so we are forced to conclude that either the earth's motion is exactly the same as the ether's (an improbable situation, to say the least) or there isn't any ether at all. One of Einstein's first great achievements in 1905 was to produce a consistent theory of light in which the concept of this ether was eliminated as superfluous.

The Michelson-Morley experiment explodes a venerable notion about empty space. Whatever else it may be, it's not filled with an ether to carry light waves. And whatever sort of wave light is, it must be able to travel across empty space without the aid of an ether.

The picture that eventually emerged from the theoretical study of light is shown in Illustration 30. Light is thought of as a

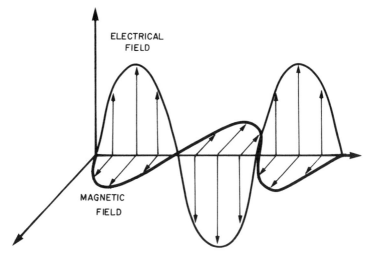

Illustration 30

set of electrical and magnetic fields, each having the form of a wave, each at a right angle to the other and to the direction of travel. It is mathematically similar to water and sound waves in that it has a regularly recurring pattern, but it differs from them in that it isn't really a wave in a medium. It is simply a wavelike entity capable of motion on its own, without an ether to support it.

One aspect of this picture of light suggests an important generalization. We have seen that different colors correspond to different wavelengths, but the human eye is sensitive only to a narrow band of wavelengths. Once we have the pictorial representation of the nature of light in mind, it is natural to ask whether there might be waves similar to light but with wavelengths that can't be seen by the human eye. The answer is yes.

There is no reason in principle why a wave of the type shown in Illustration 30 can't be produced with any wavelength at all. In fact, the wide assortment of such waves in our everyday experience makes us realize that visible light is only a special example of the more general phenomenon of electromagnetic radiation. Visible light is that portion of the spectrum to which the human eye is sensitive.

The existence of waves other than light was predicted late in the last century, and in 1890 German scientist Heinrich Hertz discovered a very important type—the radio wave. These are waves whose structure is like that pictured in Illustration 30— crossed electric and magnetic fields—but whose wavelength is anything from a few feet to many miles.

As the wavelength gets shorter, we come to microwaves (a few inches) and infrared waves (a thousandth of an inch). Visible light actually occupies only those wavelengths between 3.8×10^{-5} cm (violet) and 7.8×10^{-5} cm (red). Then, as the wavelength becomes shorter, we progress through ultraviolet, X-ray, and gamma radiation. This entire collection of possible waves is usually referred to as the electromagnetic spectrum, and it's clear that we can sense only a very small region of the spectrum directly. With our instruments, however, we can (and do) product, detect, and use the entire assortment.

Of course, if all these other forms of radiation are waves, we'd expect to see them exhibit interference just the way light does. As it turns out, they do, and this fact has had endless uses in science. To take one example, in 1912 German physicist Max von Laue did an experiment in which a beam of X-rays was directed at a crystal and then detected on the far side. The general layout is pictured in Illustration 31. The idea of the experiment is quite simple. Each atom in the crystal acts as a scatterer for the incident X-rays. For example, two neighboring atoms (like those labeled **1** and **2** in Illustration 31) will send scattered X-rays out in all directions. In general, waves arriving at a point such as that labeled A will have traveled a different distance, and this difference depends on the separation of the atoms in the crystal, a distance we have

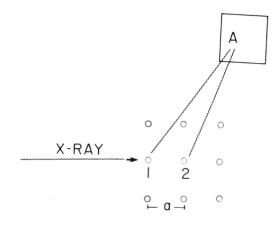

labeled *a* in the drawing. By now, you should be used to the idea that if the difference is just right, there will be constructive interference at *A*. In fact, if we develop ordinary X-ray film (the type used in hospitals), these points of constructive interference will show up as bright dots. By measuring the positions of the dots, we can infer what difference in the length of the path must exist for X-rays coming from different atoms and, from this, the separation between atoms in the crystal. Thus, the interference properties of electromagnetic waves allows us to determine the structure of solids—a technique that is widely use in research and industry today.

By the end of the nineteenth century, the wave picture of light had turned out to be not only sufficient to explain the observed phenomena, but quite useful in other fields as well. Unfortunately, there was one fly in the ointment. It was well known that if a strong light was shone on certain metals, the metal would emit electrons. This was known as the photoelectric effect, and, at first, shouldn't be surprising. After all, we know that electrons normally exist in orbits around atomic nuclei, and if light really does contain an electric field, there's no reason why it shouldn't be able to shake some electrons loose from their respective atoms. The problem isn't with the effect, however, but with the amount of time it should take to free an orbiting electron. In the wave picture of light we have just described, the interaction should be a relatively gentle process, each succeeding crest of the wave nudging the electron just a little further along on its way to freedom. The trouble is that this process ought to be slow, and there should be a span of the order of a second between the time the light is turned on and the time the electrons start coming out. In actuality, the process is practically instantaneous. The electrons start coming out as soon as the light goes on.

A solution for this problem was first suggested by Einstein in 1905 (the same year he published the special theory of relativity). He pointed out that the speed of the photoelectric effect could be understood if we assume that for some reason light acts like a particle in this sort of situation. If this is the case, then the ejection of the electron from the atoms will not be a gradual affair, but will be more like the collision of two billiard balls. The speed with which the electron is kicked out of the metal and all the other characteristics of the process are exactly explained by this picture. (One of the little-known facts in the history of science is that it was for this work, and not that on relativity, that Einstein was awarded the Nobel Prize in 1921.)

But this explanation, satisfying as it may be from the point of view of the photoelectric effect, seems to involve us in a serious contradiction with all the cases where we know that light exhibits interference and therefore acts as a wave. It would appear that a paradoxical situation has developed: to explain some things we must say that light is a wave, while to explain others we must say that it acts as a particle. In the early twentieth century, this became known as the problem of wave-particle duality.

The photoelectric effect was only the first warning bell in this field. In 1926 it was discovered that electrons, which we normally think of as particles, exhibit interference in certain circumstances. It seems that the more we learn about the basic structure of matter, the less we understand what it is!

In the 1920s, some of the more philosophically minded physicists were wondering whether or not the human mind could ever grapple with the reality of the subatomic world. More recently,

Frijthof Capra, in *The Tao of Physics* (Shambala Press, 1975), has argued that this sort of paradox means that Western science has reached the point where it has merged with Eastern religion, and that the only way we can "know" the world is through a kind of mystical enlightenment.

Well, maybe so, but my own experience as a teacher has led me to rather different conclusions. When my students in Physics 101 come to the photoelectric effect, they see no paradox at all. At first this puzzled me, but then I realized why. No one had ever told them that everything had to be either a particle or a wave. They had no reason to expect that a photon or an electron would have to be either like a baseball *or* like a ripple on a pond, so they weren't at all surprised when it wasn't. Only a professional physicist, with years of experience in dealing with objects that had to be one or the other, would have this sort of preconception.

Therefore, do photons behave as particles sometimes? Yes.

Do they behave as waves? Of course.

Then what are they? They're not particles, they're not waves, and they're not like anything you can experience directly with your senses. They are photons, and as such are like all other things that exist at the level of elementary particles.

Perhaps an analogy would make this point clear. Suppose you were a zoologist who had spent your entire professional life in North America. You would be aware of a class of things called mammals, which are warm blooded and bear their young live, and reptiles, which are cold blooded and lay eggs. You would have no trouble dealing with squirrels on the one hand and snakes on the other. But suppose you went off to Australia and discovered the duck-billed platypus. You could make one observation (measuring the blood temperature) and conclude that it is a mammal. You could make another (see whether it lays eggs or not) and conclude that it is a reptile.

Now what? Do you write learned papers on "mammal/reptile duality"? Do you despair that the human mind can ever deal with the duck-billed discovery? Do you argue that zoology has finally made contact with the mystic East and trade in your calculator for a mantra?

Well, you may, but I think most of us would agree that any of these lines of action would be pretty foolish. The proper conclusion to draw is that the new discovery simply shows that the old categories are incomplete. "Reptile/mammal" (at least as we have defined it) is a distinction that is quite reasonable if we confine our attention to North America, but fails when we go to a new region. In the same way, "wave/particle" is a reasonable distinction so long as we confine our attention to baseballs and ponds, but it fails when we start looking at things that are very small. Like the platypus, the photon and electron are new sorts of things, not assimilable in the old scheme. Their properties show us that we need new categories, but there is no reason to conclude from this that the scientific method is breaking down.

A historical example might be in order here. During the Middle Ages there was a great debate among natural philosophers over how to describe the motion of a projectile—for example, a rock thrown from your hand. According to Aristotle, there were two kinds of motion—"natural" and "violent." The problem was, how does the motion of a projectile change from violent (just as it leaves your hand) to natural (just before it hits the ground), and at what point in the trajectory does the change occur?

If you persist in describing projectile motion in these categories, then you have to admit the problem is still unsolved. Since Newton, however, physicists have taken a different approach to the problem. They say, "I can describe the path the particle will follow, where it will be, and how fast it will be moving at any time after it is thrown. This is a full description of the motion, and the classification into natural and violent is simply irrelevant." Given the success of modern science in dealing with everything from missiles to planetary probes, most of us would agree that this is a reasonable response to the medieval problem.

In the same way, a twentieth-century physicist confronted with the wave/particle duality simply points out that it is possible to predict the outcome of any experiment that can be done with electrons and photons. One does not categorize the new entities as particles or waves, any more than one categorizes motion as natural or violent. For a physicist, there is no reason to make such a categorization, and hence the entire debate about the "real" nature of elementary particles is not so much paradoxical as irrelevant. The physicist wants to ignore the problem of applying labels to the things being studied and concentrate on finding out how they actually behave.

Sounds reasonable, don't you think?

5

Why You Never See a
Rainbow in Winter

THE RAINBOW IS ONE OF THE MOST BEAUTIFUL DISPLAYS IN nature, and as such it figures prominently in folklore and mythology. In the Judaeo-Christian tradition, for example, the first rainbow appeared after the flood, and represented a promise made to Noah. In the words of the author of Genesis (9:13–15, KJV), "I do set my bow in the cloud, and it shall be for a token of a covenant between me and the earth. And it shall come to pass, when I bring a cloud over the earth, that the bow shall be seen in the cloud: And I will remember my covenant, . . . and the waters shall no more become a flood to destroy all flesh."

Since the rainbow always appears after or during a rainstorm, even the ancients realized that its appearance had something to do with sunlight and water drops. It wasn't until 1637, however, that the French philosopher-mathematician René Descartes gave the first detailed (and essentially correct) explanation of the formation of the rainbow. As it turns out, it is related to a familiar effect—the bending of light by a dense material.

There are many ways to see this effect. If you are of an experimental frame of mind, you can make a narrow beam of light by putting tape across all but a narrow slit of a flashlight lens. If you shine this beam into a water-filled aquarium, you will see something like the situation shown in Illustration 32. The beam

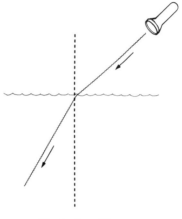

Illustration 32

will bend toward the perpendicular as it enters the water. (The only case where this won't happen is if the light is directed perpendicular to the water surface.) If you prefer not to do an experiment or don't have an aquarium handy, you can try the old Boy Scout trick of starting a fire with a magnifying glass by focusing the sun's rays on some tinder (see Illustration 33). In this case, the parallel beams of light from the sun are bent when they encounter the glass of the lens. Both of these situations involve the bending

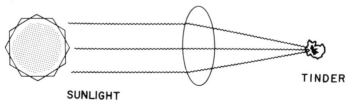

SUNLIGHT   TINDER

Illustration 33

of light rays at the interface between media of different densities, a phenomenon known as refraction.

Descartes's theory of the rainbow is based on the observation that refraction will take place when light from the sun strikes a drop of water in the air, just as light from the flashlight is bent in the experiment above. It's easiest to understand the theory if we imagine shining a small flashlight on the raindrop, choosing a flashlight that emits only one color of light. In Illustration 34 we trace the path that light would take through the drop for various positions of the flashlight. If we hold the flashlight at position *1*,

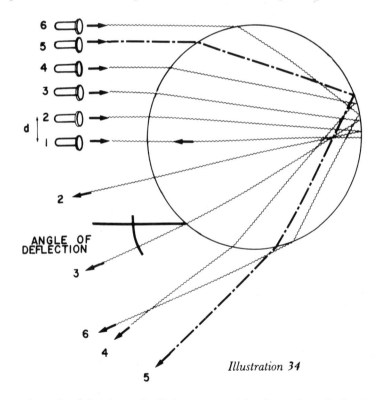

Illustration 34

on the axis of the drop, the light goes straight through to the back, is reflected, and returns without deflection to the original position. If we next move the flashlight up a distance *d* to position 2, refraction starts to become important. The light strikes the water at an angle, and is therefore bent as shown. It travels to the back of the drop, is reflected, and then is bent again when it leaves the drop. Although the light leaves the flashlight traveling in a horizontal direction, it emerges from the drop at an angle. The angle between the final and initial directions of the beam is called the angle of deflection.

If we now move the flashlight up the same distance d to position 3, the same sort of thing happens. The light that emerges from the drop is deflected even more than it was in position 2. However, it turns out that even though position 3 is twice as far from the axis as position 2, the deflection of beam 3 is not twice as much as the deflection of beam 2 but somewhat less. The same thing happens when we move up to position 4, three times as far from the axis as position 1.

The picture that emerges from this analysis, then, is this: As we move the flashlight farther and farther away from the axis, the deflection of the beam increases less and less. In other words, the deflected beams begin to "bunch up" as the flashlight is moved. Finally, this process reaches its limit at the position labeled 5, which represents the maximum angle of deflection that light can have when it encounters the drop. If we move the flashlight up still farther, for example to position 6, the beam will actually suffer less of a deflection than it did at 5. For reference, the angle of deflection corresponding to position 5 is about 42 degrees.

There are two important conclusions that we can draw from this exercise. First, all light that is scattered back from a spherical drop of water must have an angle of deflection of less than 42 degrees, and, second, because of the bunching-up effect, light from a large number of flashlight positions will be concentrated around this same 42-degree angle.

With this background we can go on to examine a situation that is a little closer to an actual rainbow. Suppose that instead of illuminating the drop with a narrow-beam flashlight, we allow a broad band of parallel beams to fall on it, keeping for the moment the restriction that the light be of one color only. This situation is shown on the left in Illustration 35. We can think of the band of parallel light as a collection of narrow beams, so the light falling

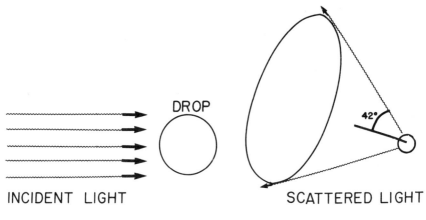

DROP

INCIDENT LIGHT

Illustration 35 (left)

42°

SCATTERED LIGHT

Illustration 35 (right)

on the drop can be considered the result of a large number of flashlights stacked in a vertical column. Then, using the results of the previous example, we can see how the drop scatters the light that hits it. Light near the axis of the drop will emerge from it at angles of less than 42 degrees. As we move away from the axis, however, the light will tend to emerge near the 42-degree angle. This means that the light that emerges from the drop can be thought of as being concentrated in a cone (shown on the right of Illustration 35) of this angle, with a diffuse illumination inside the cone. If we let this light fall on a screen, we'd see a pattern like the one shown in Illustration 36.

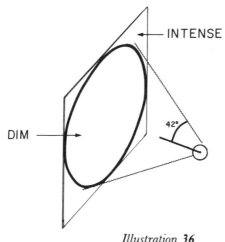

INTENSE

DIM

42°

Illustration 36

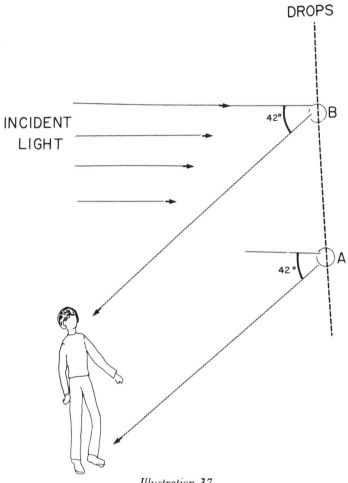

Illustration 37

Now suppose a shower of small drops is falling in the sky and they are being illuminated by a single color of light. If we stand with our backs to the light, as shown in Illustration 37, what would we see? We know that the light scattered from each drop is concentrated in a 42-degree cone, so if we look at a drop like the one labeled *A* in Illustration 37, where the angle between the incoming light and the line to our eye is less than 42 degrees, we will not see much light. We would, in fact, be looking at the dim light inside the bright cone. If, on the other hand, we looked at a drop at position *B*, where the angle *is* 42 degrees, the bright light from the cone would reach our eye, and point *B* would appear to be a bright spot in the sky.

The same argument can be made for a point that is to the right or left of the observer. In fact, any point in the sky where the angle between the incoming light and the line to the observer's eye is 42 degrees will appear bright. The net result is that there will be bright spots in the sky from each drop where this condition is met, and the sum of these bright spots will be an arc of brightness in the sky. The observer will see scattered concentrated light from every drop that lies on a 42-degree cone, as shown in Illustration 38. This is the explanation of the shape of the rainbow.

Therefore, the general configuration of the rainbow can be understood quite easily in terms of the refraction of light from

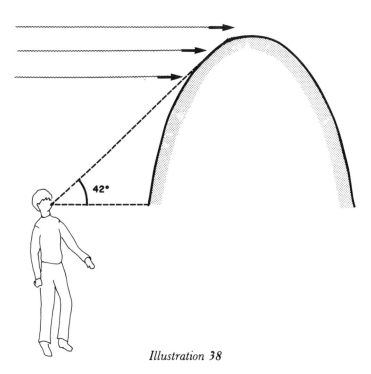

Illustration 38

water droplets in the air. But what about the most striking feature of the rainbow—its colors? Can this be understood in the same way?

The reader may have wondered why all the discussion so far has been couched in terms of a single-colored light source. The reason is quite simple: in most materials (including water), the amount of refraction varies slightly from one color to the next. This effect will be discussed in detail shortly, but for our purposes we simply note that the "magic angle" at which light is concentrated by a water drop varies from about 40 degrees (for blue) up to 42 degrees (for red). Since sunlight is a mixture of all colors in the visible spectrum, this means that each drop produces not one cone but many. As shown in Illustration 39, these cones are nested

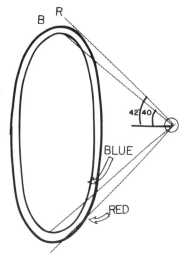

Illustration 39

inside each other. You can go through the argument above to convince yourself that this situation will give rise to a series of different-colored arcs in the sky when we view sunlight reflected from a shower of rain. Thus, the multicolored rainbow can also be understood in terms of simple physics.

One point that is implied in this explanation, but which we ought to state explicitly, is that at any instant the light from different parts of the bow is coming from different raindrops. This is depicted in Illustration 40. An observer will see a red arc at

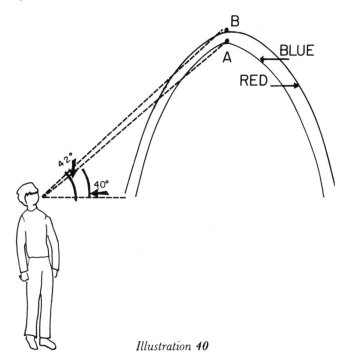

Illustration 40

point *B* (at an angle of 42 degrees) and a blue arc at point *A* (at an angle of 40 degrees), with a gradation of colors in between. Clearly, the light from these two places in the sky corresponds to emissions from two different drops. Conversely, as a single drop falls from *B* to *A*, it will contribute to different parts of the rainbow as its multicolored nested cones sweep past the eye of the observer.

With a few technical modifications, this original explanation of the rainbow has stood the test of time. The elaborations on it are too numerous to go into here, but we might point out that an interesting phenomenon, the double rainbow, can also be explained quite simply.

When light enters a raindrop there are many paths it can take other than the one we have considered. It is not too difficult to show that light following a path like the one in Illustration 41 will tend to be concentrated at an angle of 51 degrees, so that if the conditions are right we should sometimes see a double arc—the ordinary one and this one. Double rainbows are not really uncommon, of course, although they are sufficiently unusual to be worth taking time to observe when they occur. Sometimes faint extra bows can be seen inside the main arc, a phenomenon caused by interference (a process discussed in chapter 4). In fact, the only thing that you don't see is a rainbow in the winter.

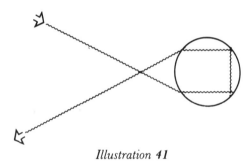

Illustration 41

The reason for this should now be obvious. The formation of the bow depends on the presence of water droplets in the air, and during the winter it doesn't rain, it snows.

Perhaps the most familiar laboratory example of the processes that give rise to a rainbow is the way an ordinary glass prism splits light into different bands of color. Newton was supposed to have been the first to use this technique to show that sunlight is made up of the entire spectrum of colors. The principle of the prism is shown in Illustration 42. Light is bent as it enters and leaves the glass, and, since red light is deflected less than violet, it will travel a different path and emerge above the path traveled by

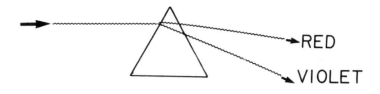

Illustration 42

the violet. Consequently, if you placed a screen to the right of the prism, you would see the rainbow effect—a shading of colors through the spectrum from red to violet. In the absence of the prism, of course, you would just see a spot of white light.

The fact that a prism will split light into its constituent colors (a property called dispersion) has been of great use to scientists in many fields. One of the important facts that was learned about atoms in the last century was that each element gives off certain well-defined wavelengths when it is heated. The most familiar example of this property is to be found in street lights. Mercury vapor lamps of the type commonly used on main streets in cities give off a bluish light, while sodium vapor, often used at highway intersections, is yellow. Thus, even the human eye can tell, under certain circumstances, which chemical elements are present in a lamp by seeing the light it gives off.

By dispersing the colors, a prism can make this sort of identification much more precise. If we were to shine a mercury vapor lamp on a prism as shown in Illustration 43, we would not see a bluish smear on the screen, but a series of very narrow lines. (We see lines because we send the light through a slit.) If the lamp were sodium, we would see an entirely different set of lines. A mercury lamp looks faintly blue to us because, although many colors are present, the blue line is most intense. Similarly, the sodium yellow lines overpower the other colors when viewed with the naked eye. Just why each atom gives off the colors it does is one of the main fields of study in atomic physics.

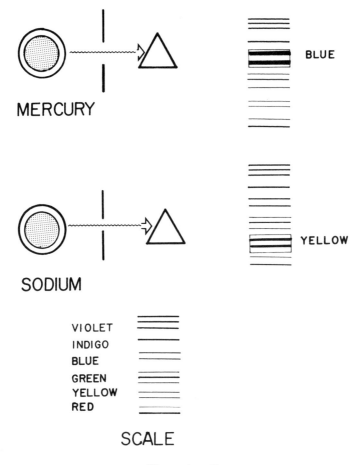

Illustration 43

Such a collection of lines is called the spectrum of the element being tested, and the lines themselves are called spectral lines. No matter where the source of light is, if it contains mercury or sodium the same lines will be seen when light from that source is sent through a prism. The implications for astronomy are far-reaching, because the prism will act in the same way whether the light entering it comes from a laboratory lamp or a distant star. In either case it will unfailingly produce a spectrum that can be analyzed to show the elements that produced the light. And by comparing the intensities of the lines associated with one element with those associated with another, the relative abundance of the two elements in the source can be determined. So potent is the technique that until very recently we knew more about the chemical composition of distant stars—even stars in other galaxies—than about the planets and moons of our own solar system, which shine with reflected light.

The prism has another interesting property besides its use as a spectrometer. If you hold a prism in front of a white surface and shine a beam of light up into it at an angle, the light will emerge and form an image toward the bottom. If you move the source up, the image will move up as well until you reach a certain critical angle (the path labeled *C* in Illustration 44). Moving the source

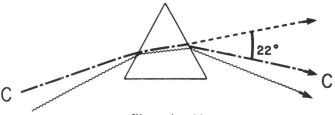

Illustration 44

up beyond this point results in the image's moving down again. This behavior is not too different from what we sketched for the raindrop earlier (Illustration 34), and, by a similar line of reasoning, we should expect a concentration of the light striking a face of the prism at the angle corresponding to the path *C*. For reference, the path *C* for a prism with 60-degree angles at the corners involves a total deflection of the incident light by an angle of about 22 degrees. This means that if there were a collection of prisms in the air, we would expect them to form a bow whose angular size was 22 degrees.

We saw that rainbows don't appear in winter because water freezes. What if we take this one step further and ask what the ice will do when sunlight hits it? We all know that snowflakes (one sort of frozen water) are six-sided. The exact shape of an ice crystal depends on the conditions at the moment of freezing, but the two most common shapes (other than snowflakes) are a long, thin, pencillike column with six sides and a flat hexagon, like a six-sided stop sign.

If sunlight should strike the side of a pencil-shaped crystal, it would follow a path like the one shown in Illustration 45. In fact,

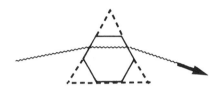

Illustration 45

as far as the light is concerned, the ice crystal is identical to a prism whose corners are 60 degrees each. We have extended the sides of the crystal with dotted lines to show its similarity to a prism. This means that if the ice crystals are in the air and falling so that the sunlight hits the long sides, the light that comes through will tend to be concentrated at an angle of 22 degrees. If you are standing and looking at the sun (or the moon, for that matter) through a collection of such crystals (see Illustration 46), you will see a bright circle centered at the sun having an angular size of 22 degrees. (The arguments leading to this conclusion are identical to those that led to the 42-degree rainbow.) This is the so-called 22-degree halo that can be seen around the sun or the moon in clear, cold weather. It differs from the rainbow in that the bright light you see is transmitted through the crystal, rather than scattered back from the droplet. In the Midwest, where I grew up, a halo around the moon was supposed to mean that there would be snow the next day. This bit of meteorological lore may or may not be true, but such a halo does indicate the presence of ice crystals in the air.

The 22-degree halo, although the most familiar effect of the interaction of light with ice crystals, is only one of a large number

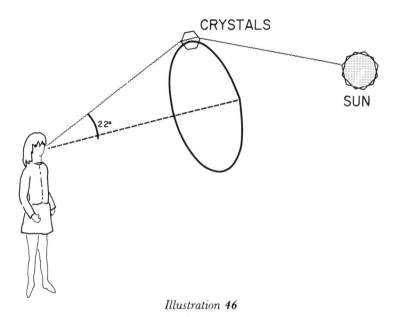

CRYSTALS

SUN

22°

Illustration 46

of such displays. In his excellent book *Rainbows, Halos and Glories* (Cambridge University Press, 1980), Robert Greenler lists no fewer than twenty-two effects that have been seen in the sky because of the presence of various kinds and orientations of crystals. For example, "sun dogs" (bright spots seen level with the sun and 22 degrees away from it) are caused by light going through flat crystals as shown on the left in Illustration 47. Sun pillars (a

Illustration 47 (left)   *Illustration 47* (right)

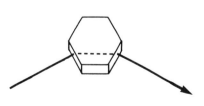

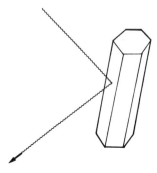

column of light above the sun) are caused by reflection from the long side of pencil-shaped crystals falling end on as shown on the right of Illustration 47. There are many ways light can interact with these two types of crystals, and this is the reason for the large number of possible displays.

There is another interesting aspect to this topic. Robert Greenler is an atmospheric physicist at the University of Wisconsin–Milwaukee. Part of his interest in displays has to do with what he calls sky archaeology. We know that in the past many strange things have been seen in the sky, and these are sometimes recorded, either in mythology or in astronomical writings. For example, on February 20, 1661, a complex series of arcs appeared in the sky over Gdansk, Poland. Where these arcs intersected each other there were bright spots. There were seven intersections; so this came to be known as the "seven suns" display. It was recorded by the astronomer Hevelius, so we have an accurate record of its appearance. Similarly, in Russia, on June 18, 1790, there appeared a complex series of arcs with six apparent suns in the sky over St. Petersburg—a display that lasted from 7:30 A.M. until just past noon. Both of these were very unusual and complex phenomena, but Greenler, with the aid of some computer simulation, was able to show how each (as well as some more modern ones) could be produced by a particular mixture of ice crystals in the sky.

This may seem to be an interesting but not very timely result. Few people have heard of the original displays, after all, so being able to explain them is unlikely to be front-page news.

This would be so if it were not for the fact that during the past few decades, several well-publicized pseudoscientific theories have been published that depend very heavily on an appeal to historical records of unusual celestial events. The granddaddy of these scenarios was published by Immanuel Velikovsky in *Worlds in Collision* in 1950. Basing his arguments on astronomical events recorded in ancient writings—for example, the account of the sun standing still in the heavens, which we find in the Book of Joshua—he claimed that within historical times the planet Venus was ejected from Jupiter, bounced around the solar system for a while causing spectacular celestial events, and finally settled into its present orbit. More recently, Eric von Daniken's *Chariots of the Gods* joined the display of intellectual foolishness, again using arguments based partially on recorded instances of unusual celestial events. And of course, the daily UFO sightings can be added to this list, if you wish.

All of these "theories" have one thing in common—an unspoken assumption that unusual events must have unusual explanations, particularly if those events involve some sort of celestial display. But logic demands that before we accept a far-fetched explanation, we convince ourselves that the events cannot have a more mundane origin. This is where work like Greenler's plays such an important role, for it shows us how spectacular and unusual events can have explanations that rest on simple physical principles.

For example, the seven suns over Gdansk that we described is at least as spectacular as any of the events Velikovsky uses to "prove" his thesis. We can imagine that if this display occurred a few thousand years earlier in a civilization without an advanced knowledge of astronomy, some chronicler would have recorded it in mythological terms, perhaps as a battle taking place between the sun god and his children. It would be fun to see how Velikovsky and his followers would have tried to explain this in terms of the wandering of the planet Venus. Von Daniken would no doubt have claimed it was the record of a battle in space. But, because we are lucky enough to have precise records of the actual event, we can explain it in relatively simple terms, without having to suspend either the laws of celestial mechanics, as Velikovsky would have us do, or the laws of common sense, as we would have to do to accept ancient astronauts.

Of course, this argument against the credibility of pseudo-scientific accounts of historic events is based purely on the laws of physics. One scientist, quoted in *Astronomy* magazine, pointed out another. "If you want to believe these accounts," he said, "you have to believe that ancient authors never lied, never exaggerated, and never used hyperbole to make their accounts seem more important. The violations of the laws of human nature involved in this belief make the violations of the laws of physics pale in comparison."

So the next time you get trapped at a cocktail party by someone who claims that Ezekiel's wheel was really a spaceship or that the manna that fed the Israelites was really part of the atmosphere of the planet Venus, remember how much can be explained just by thinking about the way sunlight interacts with a prism.

6

Why Won't a Magnet Pick Up Pennies?

MAGNETISM HAS ALWAYS SEEMED TO ME THE MOST MYSTERIOUS force in nature. I remember a particularly vivid dream I had as a graduate student in which I suddenly had an insight that not only allowed me to use the equations of magnetism, but allowed me to *understand*—to see how magnetism fits into the entire cosmic scheme. Unfortunately, when I woke up I remembered the dream but couldn't recover the insight, so I had to keep studying the subject in the conventional way. I used to think I was the only physicist who felt this way about magnetism, but I recently heard a talk by Nobel Laureate Edward M. Purcell of Harvard University, and he, too, confessed to a sense of mystery when thinking about magnets.

Perhaps I can communicate some of this feeling to you by describing a few things you can do with ordinary bar magnets. You know that either end of a bar magnet will pick up iron objects like nails, but that the magnet won't attract things made from aluminum or copper. If you wrap your hand around the magnet, it will still pick up the nails. Whatever magnetism is, it will go right through your body. You can turn a nail into a magnet by stroking it with another magnet, but if you heat the nail the magnetic effects will vanish. If you float a bar magnet on a cork in a pan of water, it will line up in a north–south direction (this is the principle of the compass). The end of the magnet that points north is called the north pole. If you bring the north pole of one magnet near the south pole of another, the two magnets will stick together. If you bring the north pole of one near the north pole of another, they will be repelled by each other. Given all these effects (which constitute just a small part of the phenomenon we call magnetism), it's not hard to justify the term *mysterious*.

Perhaps the best way to discuss magnets is to think about the compass. Since magnets are known to exert forces on one another, the easiest way to explain the alignment of a compass needle is to suppose that the earth itself is a giant magnet, differing from the standard dime-store variety only in size and strength. If this is the case, then a magnet placed somewhere on the surface of the earth will feel two forces (see Illustration 48): The north pole of the magnet will be pulled toward the south magnetic pole of the earth, and the south pole of the magnet will be pulled toward the north magnetic pole of the earth. Both of these forces will tend to twist the small magnet around until it aligns itself in a north–south direction.

There is a somewhat sticky point of nomenclature here that has to be cleared up. We know that the north pole of one magnet will repel the north pole of another. Consequently, if we call the north-pointing end of the compass needle the north pole of the compass, we have to conclude that the south pole of the terrestrial magnet lies in Greenland. By usage (and geography), however, the magnetic pole in Greenland is referred to as the earth's north magnetic pole. Since this is an eminently sensible terminology, we'll use it even if it does cause occasional confusion.

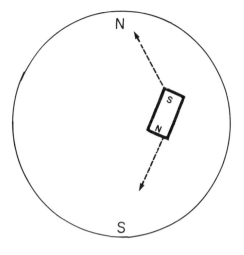

Illustration 48

With a compass it is possible to map out the magnetic field surrounding any magnet, including that which envelops the earth. All we have to do is lay a small compass down near the earth's pole and note the position of its head and tail. We can then lay a second compass next to the first, with the head of the second next to the tail of the first. If we keep adding compasses in this way (see Illustration 49), we begin to see a single line forming. If we then drew a map of all the different lines we could trace near the

Illustration 49

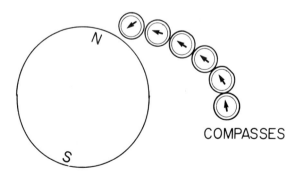

COMPASSES

earth in this way, we'd get a picture like that on the left in Illustration 50. If we did the same around an ordinary magnet, we'd get a picture like that on the right in Illustration 50. The similarity between these two patterns is striking. The characteristic magnetic

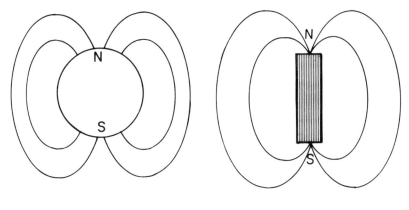

Illustration 50 (left)   *Illustration 50* (right)

field pattern shown is always associated with magnets possessing two poles (north and south) and for that reason is called a dipole field. All known natural magnets produce dipole fields.

If we leave the description of magnetic effects and begin to ask what the causes of magnetism are, we are forced to confront a yet more mysterious fact. A compass needle placed near a wire carrying an electric current will be deflected, just as it would be by the earth or any other magnet. This basic fact leads to the unification of electricity and magnetism, as we will see in chapter 12. If a long wire carries current along it, then the magnetic field associated with the wire will be a series of concentric circles, as shown on the left in Illustration 51. If the wire carrying the electrical current is bent into a loop, however, then the magnetic field will be as shown on the right. It will, in fact, be of the familiar dipole type.

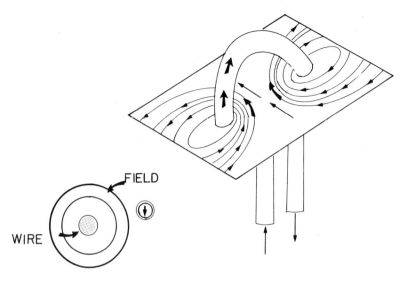

FIELD

WIRE

Illustration 51 (left) *Illustration 51* (right)

That a loop of wire carrying an electric current can produce a dipole field means that for all intents and purposes the loop can be thought of as a simple magnet with the customary north and south poles. There are important practical implications of this fact, as we shall see shortly, but this statement is even more important in our quest for a deep understanding of magnetism. The reason will become obvious if you think about the simple atom in Illustration 52. As we all know, the atom consists of a small nucleus

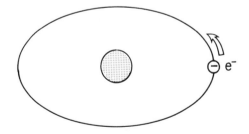

e⁻

Illustration 52

surrounded by orbiting electrons. For simplicity, we'll consider an atom with only one electron, but our conclusions can be extended to more complicated atoms as well. The point is this: An electron going in a circle around the nucleus *is* a current loop. The best way to see this is to go back and look at an ordinary current-carrying wire. If we look closely enough, we see many millions of

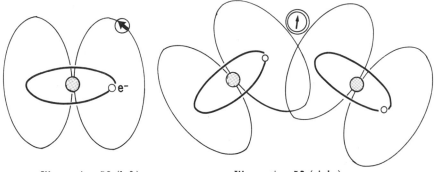

Illustration 53 (left)   *Illustration 53* (right)

electrons running through the wire, colliding with atoms and producing all the effects we associate with electrical current. If we start to turn the current down, the only thing we see is a diminution in the number of moving electrons. If we take this process to its logical conclusion, we have a current made up of a single electron. This, of course, is just what we have in an atom.

As far as magnetic effects are concerned, then, each atom can be thought of as a tiny bar magnet, and a collection of atoms would, in general, look like a set of small magnets in random orientations.

This is all we really need to understand magnetism. Imagine placing a microscopic compass near a single atom, as shown on the left in Illustration 53. The compass will align itself with the magnetic field produced by that atom. Next, imagine that a second atom is brought up, as shown on the right in Illustration 53. The compass needle will now orient itself so as to reflect the influence of both atoms. Technically, we say that the needle points in the direction of the sum of the two atomic magnetic fields. In general, the orientation of the second atom will be completely random with regard to the first, so that the composite magnetic field seen by the compass is as likely to be increased as it is to be decreased by the presence of the second atom. If we now add in the billions of atoms whose magnetic fields could be expected to influence our compass in a real material, it's not too hard to see that adding up so many randomly oriented magnetic fields will tend to wash everything out, leaving little or no net magnetic field for the compass to detect. For most materials, this is exactly what happens.

For a few materials, however, there is another property that becomes important. In these materials forces exist that tend to cause the atoms to line up so that the atomic magnets, instead of being oriented randomly in space, all wind up pointing in the same direction. In these materials the compass deflections due to individual atoms, instead of offsetting each other as in the example above, combine to produce a single, very large magnetic field. The large magnetic field we find outside an ordinary bar magnet results from the cumulative effect of the aligned atomic magnets inside of it.

This point having been made, it is necessary to add a few caveats. In the first place, the force that causes the atomic magnets in iron to align themselves is not itself magnetic. It arises from other forces between the atoms that are much stronger than any magnetic force that exists on the atomic level. Whether this force does or does not exist in a given material seems to depend very precisely on the details of the way the material is put together. In order to get the alignment, there has to be a certain amount of free space between the atoms in a solid—too much or too little and the alignment disappears. This is why only a few elements—iron, cobalt, nickel, and some compounds made from them—can be used to make permanent magnets.

The second problem with the description we've given is that it seems to imply that every atomic dipole in a piece of magnetic material must point in the same direction. In fact, the alignment process takes place on a much smaller scale. If you were able to see into a piece of iron, you would see that there are tiny volumes (about the size of a grain of sand) in which all the atoms are lined up. These volumes are called domains. While the dipoles in a given domain may point in one direction, the dipoles in the next may point in another, so that, in general, the alignment of two neighboring volumes will not be the same.

The reason that many domains are formed in a piece of iron has to do with the fact that every system in nature tends toward a state of lowest possible energy (see chapter 3). Suppose we have a piece of iron in which there are N domains. If we know the energy of this system, we can ask whether the energy of a state with one more domain is higher or lower. If it is lower, then the system will evolve to a state with $N + 1$ domains. If it is higher, the system will stay where it is.

Creating an extra domain involves two energy-consuming processes. We must order the atoms to create the domain, and we must put energy into the magnetic field associated with the total collection of domains. If we have a small number of domains, the creation energy is minimized, but, because there are only a few magnetic fields to cancel each other out, the energy of the field will be high. Conversely, if we create a large number of domains the magnetic effects will tend to cancel, which means that the energy in the field is small, but we have to expend a lot of energy to create the domains in the first place. Clearly, there is some optimum number of domains where the tradeoff between these two effects minimizes the total energy, and this is the state to which the system will evolve.

The picture that emerges from this discussion is shown in Illustration 54. In a normal nonmagnetic piece of iron, the domains point in random directions. Using arguments similar to that given for the case where individual atoms are aligned at random, we can demonstrate that the magnetic field due to all the randomly oriented domains will be almost zero. Thus, a normal piece of iron is not a magnet. If, however, something happens to cause all the domains to line up, as shown on the right in Illustra-

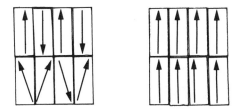

Illustration 54

tion 54, then someone outside the material will see a strong magnetic field and will conclude that the sample is indeed a permanent magnet.

The process of magnetization, then, proceeds via two steps. First, the interatomic forces act to form the domains and align the atomic dipoles within each one, and then some other agency acts to align the domains to make a magnet. When you stroke a nail with a magnet and the nail itself turns into a second magnet, what you are doing is aligning the domains in the iron of the nail. If you heat the nail, the energy added by the flame scrambles the alignment you induced and the end result is an ordinary nail again, without any magnetic properties.

The connection between heating and atomic alignment played an important role in one of the most important discoveries in twentieth-century geology—the concept of continental drift. Although the idea that the continents float around on the earth's mantle had been around since the 1920s, it had generally been discounted for lack of evidence. In recent times, magnetic evidence has provided striking support for the theory of continental drift.

If Europe and North America are really moving apart, as the theory suggests, then there must be some fissure in the middle of the Atlantic Ocean where the crust of the earth is split apart so that hot magma from underneath can come to the surface (see Illustration 55). The upwelling material is molten, but after a time it will cool off and solidify. Atoms and molecules in a liquid are

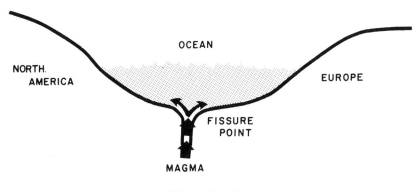

Illustration 55

free to move about, so we would expect no alignment of the atomic magnets when the magma first comes to the surface. In this sense, the magma is like the heated nail in the above example, exhibiting magnetic properties only when it cools off. If a magnetic material solidifies in the presence of an external magnetic field, the atomic magnets will tend to align themselves with that field. In the case of the upwelling magma, there should be a tendency for the atoms to be aligned in the direction of the earth's magnetic field.

It is a well-established (though poorly understood) fact that the earth's magnetic field reverses itself at irregular intervals, so that at some periods in the past a compass would have pointed south instead of north. If the continents really are separating and tearing apart the ocean floor, the magnetic alignment of materials near the midocean fissure would be something like that in Illustration 56. Looking down at the ocean floor, we would see the rock nearest the fissure (i.e., the material that has come to the surface most recently) with a magnetization directed toward the present North Pole. As we moved away from the fissure, we would suddenly detect a change in the direction of magnetism. The rock in which the magnetization points south must have solidified before the last reversal of the earth's field 700,000 years ago. Moving still farther from the fissure, we would see another reversal. The magnetization would again point north, and so on. The characteristic pattern of bands of alternating direction could only arise from the

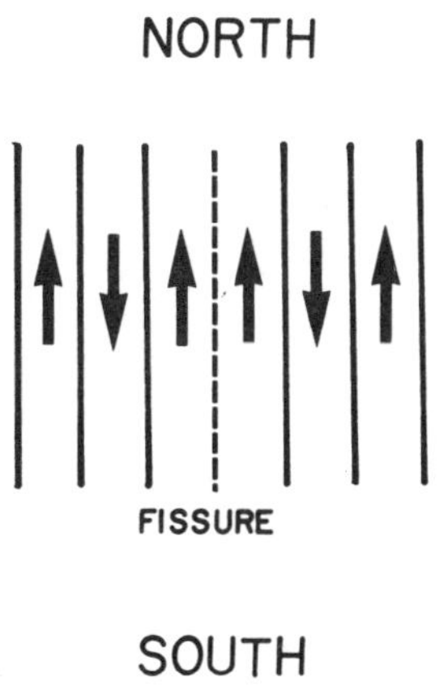

NORTH

FISSURE

SOUTH

Illustration 56

separation of the continents in an environment with an alternating magnetic field.

The idea of atomic magnetism allows us to answer the question that is the title of this chapter. A magnet won't pick up pennies because pennies are made of copper. The amount of space between atoms in metallic copper doesn't happen to be just the right amount needed to form domains, so, although each individual copper atom is a small magnet, there is no large-scale magnetism associated with their orientation. Consequently, there is no large interaction between the field of the magnet and a penny, and the force of gravity keeps the penny on the table.

Perhaps the most intriguing thing about this answer is the implication that *every* magnet, natural or synthetic, exists because of the motion of an electron somewhere. In the case of a natural magnet, it is the electrons going around nuclei in atoms that give rise to magnetic effects (although that requires the intermediate step of domain creation). For many everyday applications another kind of magnet device—the electromagnet—is used, but the same principle applies. An electromagnet is like the loop of wire we talked about earlier. When an electric current flows, the loop produces the same field as a dipole magnet, but with the added advantage that the strength of the magnet can be controlled by adjusting the current. But even here, the source of the magnetism is a collection of electrons moving in the wire.

Even large-scale magnetic fields, like those associated with the earth and the sun, are thought to have their origin in charges in motion. That the earth has a magnetic field, for example, is supposed to be intimately tied to the fact that part of the core of the earth is liquid iron that is free to move around. We could think of this as a sort of current loop, although the periodic shifts in the earth's field mean that the correct description of terrestrial magnetism must be more complicated than the simple correspondence between a loop and a dipole magnet. There has been a good deal of theoretical work on this problem, but we still do not have a totally satisfactory understanding of the details of how the field is generated, although the broad outlines are known.

That every magnetic field is related to a moving electrical charge points to one of the great mysteries in modern physics. There is a high level of symmetry between electrical and magnetic effects in nature. Purely electrical phenomena, such as charges in motion, can give rise to magnetic fields. It is also possible for purely magnetic phenomena to produce electrical fields. When physicists see this sort of symmetry in nature, they have a strong tendency to believe that the symmetry should be complete—that *every* electrical effect should be mirrored by a magnetic one and vice versa.

But there is one aspect of this hypothetical symmetry that simply fails to hold. We find in nature objects like the electron that can, in and of themselves, exert electrical forces. These electrical forces are completely independent of any magnetic effects. At this point the symmetry between electricity and magnetism breaks down, because, as we have seen, *all* magnetic effects are the result of electrical currents. There is no magnetic equivalent of the electrical charge.

The idea that nature would be almost, but not quite, symmetrical is anathema to most theoretical physicists. All our experience leads us to expect that when we find a fundamental theory, it will be aesthetically pleasing as well as correct. Of course, that this has been true in the past is no guarantee that it must be true in the future, but it does create a strong motive to search for the elements that are missing from the present picture and that would, if found, produce exactly the kind of symmetry we expect.

The magnetic effects we have discussed so far all deal with the magnetic dipole. Every magnetic field we know about ultimately derives from magnets that have both a north and a south pole. A magnetic "charge" would correspond to a magnet that had only one pole, and hence, it is usually referred to as a "magnetic monopole." The way that physicists usually state the conclusion that magnetic effects in nature arise from electrical currents is to say that magnetic monopoles do not exist. These two statements are logically equivalent.

So, the quest for beauty and symmetry in nature comes down to a search for an isolated magnetic pole. Until quite recently, the primary motive for these searches had to do with the type of "philosophical" arguments we have just gone through. More recently, scientists working on unified field theories (see chapter 12) have found that many versions of these theories seem to predict the existence of monopoles. This, of course, adds fresh motives for the search.

The experiments that have been done along these lines can be split into two categories: direct searches and geological searches. Direct searches are made by letting a beam of high-energy particles (either from an accelerator or from cosmic rays) hit a target and then examining the debris of the collision to see if some of the energy of the projectile has been converted into the mass required to make a magnetic monopole. These experiments are routinely done whenever a new accelerator is inaugurated on the off chance that something may turn up, but they have been uniformly unsuccessful up to now. A variation of this type of search involves examining the cosmic rays that fall on the earth to see if any of them are magnetic monopoles. This has the advantage that it is not necessary to create the particles before they are detected, so that magnetic monopoles created in distant supernovas or others left over from the Big Bang might be seen.

The geological searches operate on the assumption that once monopoles have been created somewhere and come into the solar system, those that strike the earth or moon will be trapped in the atomic magnetic fields of rocks near the surface. Thus, even if the number of monopoles that hit the earth in any given year is small, in the billions of years that the earth has been around a lot of them should have accumulated in surface material. Blocks of ice from the North and South poles, moon rocks, and a variety of other materials have been examined without any positive result.

On Sunday, February 14, 1982 (St. Valentine's Day), Stanford physicist Blas Cabrera recorded what may well be the first experimental evidence for the existence of magnetic poles. Using a radically new method of detection, he measured an event that, in all probability, was the passage of a cosmic ray monopole through his apparatus. While there is still some debate about his experiment, and while no further monopoles have been detected as of this writing, interest in magnetic monopoles among physicists has increased significantly over the last year. If Cabrera is proved right, it will show that it is sometimes important for scientists to trust to their instincts about the inherent beauty and symmetry of nature, waiting for the proper experiment to justify their faith.

7

The Thermometer
and the Atom

DAILY USAGE HAS MADE THE CONCEPT OF TEMPERATURE FAMIL-
iar to everyone. Whether we are listening to a weather report, setting a dial on an oven, or visiting the doctor, temperature is a part
of our lives. But when we are forced to go beyond this easy asso-
ciation and give a precise definition of temperature, we find that
we face a difficult problem. First, we must find a way of assigning
numbers to the different environments that we say are at different
temperatures, determining by some test that one environment is
hotter than another. After that we must find some fundamental
understanding of what temperature is, rather than just how to give
it a number. Since we know that heat is related to the motion of
atoms (see chapter 1), we might expect that the search for the ultimate definition of temperature will eventually lead us into the
microscopic world.

One of the most surprising aspects of the history of our ideas about temperature is the complete lack of any quantitative method of dealing with it until quite recently. We know that the Greeks had developed some basic notions about the science of heat. Hero of Alexandria developed the first working model of a steam engine, although it was more a toy than a tool. Although the Greeks obviously had the same sort of sensations that we do on hot days, and although the weather was as important to them as to us, they had no way of saying in a quantitative way just how hot (or cold) it was on a given day.

In fact, the first thermometer wasn't built until the seventeenth century. Galileo is remembered today for his contributions to the science of mechanics and astronomy and, perhaps with less justification, for his heresy trial. It is not widely known that he also spent a good deal of his time applying his considerable talents to developing practical devices. It is a measure of his talent in this direction that his invention of one of the first thermometers in 1602 is skipped over in all but the most detailed biographies.

A sketch of Galileo's thermometer is shown in Illustration 57.

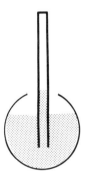

Illustration 57

It consisted of a narrow glass tube about 22 inches long, which was closed at one end, and a bowl of colored water. To take a reading, you would remove the glass tube from the apparatus and hold it in your hand to warm it up. While still warming the glass, you would put it into the bowl. As the glass cooled off to room temperature, the air inside would contract and water would rise in the tube. The height of the rise would be a measure of the temperature of the surroundings.

You may have realized already that this is not a very good thermometer. The height to which the water rises in the tube actually depends on two things—the volume of the trapped air, which depends on the temperature, and the atmospheric pressure, which pushes on the water in the bowl and balances the force of gravity on the water in the tube. Thus, Galileo's thermometer could display a change of temperature when the air around it got warmer, but it could also do so if the atmospheric pressure changed, as it does regularly when weather systems move by. This attempt to quantify the idea of temperature resulted in something that bore a greater resemblance to a barometer than it does to a modern thermometer.

Nevertheless, this first design provided the basis for improvements. The first thermometer in which the entire working apparatus—tube plus bowl—were in a sealed glass container to eliminate the effects of atmospheric pressure appeared in 1653 and was brought into general use by Duke Ferdinand II of Tuscany. By 1670 the mercury thermometer was developed in pretty much its present form. By the end of the seventeenth century, the simple kinds of thermometers we now use to measure body temperature and to keep track of the weather outside our door were already in existence.

The kinds of thermometers we have described (and, indeed, all other types as well) do not measure the quantity we call temperature directly, but rather some other quantity that is known to vary as heat is injected into or extracted from a material. In the familiar mercury thermometer, for example, we make use of the fact that when a material is heated it expands in volume. Anyone who has watched a saucepan of milk boil over on the stove is familiar with this. Since the mercury is confined in a glass tube, the only way that this expansion can take place is for the mercury to rise in the tube, resulting in the familiar line whose top corresponds to the temperature.

Once the principle of the working thermometer was established, the next task facing researchers was the establishment of a temperature scale—a way of assigning numbers to the readings on the thermometers. In the seventeenth century, instrument makers usually attached glass beads at regular intervals to the sides of the thermometer tubes to save users the bother of measuring the height of the fluid with a ruler. While this was undoubtedly an improvement over previous procedures, it still left a rather unsettling situation, where the temperature being read depended on the particular instrument being used.

Perhaps the best way to understand the problem involved is to imagine two researchers in different laboratories measuring a particular chemical reaction and then comparing notes. Suppose they discover that the temperatures they measured aren't the same. Is this because the experiments differed from each other, or because they were using different thermometers? Without an agreement on how to go about assigning numbers to a temperature scale, there would be no way of answering this question. Worse yet, even if they agreed on the temperature they measured, they couldn't be sure that the reactions weren't actually happening at different temperatures, and that the difference was being compensated by the differences between their thermometers.

Therefore, even such a simple operation as comparing experiments done in different places with different instruments requires the establishment of a temperature scale. One way to proceed is to define two easily reproducible environments—common modern choices are the freezing and boiling points of water—and then define a degree of temperature as some fraction of the difference of the heights of the column of mercury between the two environments.

The first attempt at establishing a universal scale of this type was made in 1701 by the Danish astronomer Olaus Roemer. He thought all temperature readings should be positive numbers, so he labeled the coldest mixture he could produce in the laboratory (a mixture of salt and freezing water) as zero degrees of temperature. He called the boiling point of water 60 degrees, so that the freezing point of water worked out to be 7½ degrees. (For some reason it was important to him to have one-eighth of his temperature scale below freezing.)

About the same time, an instrument maker in Amsterdam named Daniel Gabriel Fahrenheit became interested in making thermometers. The development of the familiar Fahrenheit scale of temperature is one of those amusing stories that is often overlooked in the history of science because it shows that scientists, like other mortals, can make mistakes.

Fahrenheit was aware of Roemer's work, and began by adapting it to his own manufacturing business. In describing his upper temperature standard, Roemer used the German word *blutwarm*, which translates literally as *blood warm*. Roemer used this word in the sense of *hot*, but Fahrenheit thought he was referring to the temperature of the human body. Consequently, when he began working out his own temperature scale, he chose one based on human body temperature (which he called 22½ degrees) and melting ice (7½ degrees). It quickly became apparent to him that these numbers were not particularly easy to use, and in 1717 he changed them to 96 and 32 degrees, respectively, "to avoid inconvenient and awkward fractions."

Using this scale, Fahrenheit measured the boiling point of water to be 212 degrees, and he published this result. As the scale came to be adopted, it proved to be much easier to calibrate thermometers by using the freezing and boiling of water as standards, rather than the temperature of the human body. Unfortunately, Fahrenheit's measurement of the boiling point of water was wrong. As better thermometers became available, it was found that if the boiling point of water was taken to be 212 degrees and the freezing point to be 32 degrees, then human body temperature is 98.6 degrees not 96. This, of course, is the number familiar to us all.

How could Fahrenheit have made such an error? The answer to this question illustrates an important point about the nature of science, so it's worth considering it in some detail. As we have already seen, early thermometers were based on the fact that materials expand in a uniform manner when heated. For example, if a temperature change of 10 degrees causes a certain increase in volume of a material, then a change of 20 degrees will cause twice that increase. If we think of a mercury thermometer, and if we assume that the diameter of the glass tube is exactly the same everywhere, as illustrated in the thermometer on the left in Illustration 58, then these uniform changes in volume will translate

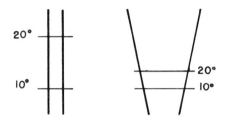

Illustration 58

into uniform changes in the height of the mercury column. This is why the degree markings on a thermometer are evenly spaced. If, however, the glass tube is not of uniform diameter, this will not be true. An extreme case of nonuniformity is shown on the right in Illustration 58. It is clear that equal changes in the total volume of the mercury will result in unequal changes in the height of the column, since it takes a higher volume of mercury to produce equal changes in height as we move up the tube.

This is probably the cause of Fahrenheit's difficulty. He lived at a time when it simply was not technically possible to produce a glass tube with a sufficiently uniform bore to serve as an accurate thermometer. The lesson we can learn from this historical incident is that very often the progress of science depends on our ability to carry out seemingly grubby and unimportant tasks. We don't know who the person was who first figured out how to make a glass tube with a uniform diameter from one end to the other. In fact, this feat was probably not due to one person at all, but to the cumulative efforts of many artisans toiling in anonymity. Yet without their work it would have been impossible to establish reliable temperature scales, and the entire science of thermodynamics—one of the cornerstones of modern physics—could not have been developed. It appears, then, that science is more like a football game than a tennis match. Superstars are important, and they're the people with the highest visibility. But even the best running back wouldn't get very far without the help of the unsung linemen who do the blocking. Like the linemen in football, the "linemen" in science seldom get much recognition.

Despite these early difficulties, the Fahrenheit temperature scale came into widespread use and is still common in North America. In 1742 the Swedish astronomer Anders Celsius proposed that the interval between the freezing and boiling points of water should encompass only 100 degrees. It is a little-known historical fact that he originally "stood the temperature scale on its head" by calling boiling 0 degrees and freezing 100 degrees, but others quickly put things right side up and produced the familiar Celsius, or centigrade, scale. This scale is used throughout much of the world and is generally associated with the metric system.

One thing should be clear from the history of the Fahrenheit and Celsius systems, however. There is no such thing as a "correct" or "right" temperature scale. Each step in the development of a scale is totally arbitrary, involving a choice based more on convenience than any overriding scientific principle. The use of water to establish the two ends of the scales we use today is reasonable, since water is a commonly available substance. But there is no reason in principle why the interval between boiling and freezing should not be 1,000 degrees rather than 100 or 180. Similarly, there is no reason why substances other than water shouldn't be used to define the scale. Why not use the boiling and melting points of iron, for example? I have been told that some old breweries in Europe used a scale based on the boiling and freezing points of alcohol until after World War II.

It is possible to argue that in many ways the Fahrenheit scale is much better suited to everyday use than the Celsius. For one thing, the Fahrenheit degree is roughly half as big as the Celsius degree, which means that if we use the Fahrenheit scale it is possible to achieve greater accuracy in reporting temperatures without resorting to decimals. This is a particular advantage in meteorology and weather forecasting, where whole-number temperature readings are customarily used. And for all its accidental history, the Fahrenheit scale is much more psychologically suited to weather forecasting (where people use temperature most often in the normal course of affairs) than the Celsius. There is a special, almost magical, significance attached to situations in which the number of digits in a number changes. Feeling like a million dollars seems more exuberant than feeling like $900,000. Similarly, when the temperature reaches 100 degrees Fahrenheit, the idea of heat is conveyed more dramatically than if we were to say it is 37.7 degrees Centigrade. Like so much of the English system of measure, the Fahrenheit scale is geared to the human being. This is one reason why I feel that the present push to convert to metric units in the United States is, at the very least, misguided.

In any case, the establishment of universally accepted scales removes some of the arbitrariness from the measurement of temperature. Now, if two different laboratories do the same experiment and get different results for a temperature, at least we now know that the difference is real. But in a deeper sense, the Fahrenheit and centigrade scales as we've defined them up to now are not *truly* universal. Even though the two end points of the temperature scale are unambiguously defined, measuring any temperature in between depends on the expansion properties of the specific material used.

In general, the amount that a material expands when its temperature changes by one degree depends slightly on the temperature of the material before heating. For example, a foot-long bar of iron at room temperature (20°C, 68°F) will expand .00014 inches if its temperature is raised one degree C, while a foot-long bar at the boiling point of water will expand .00016 inches. Irregularities of this sort are different for different materials, so any temperature scale defined by the expansion of a given material will depend on the detailed properties of that material. This should not be the case with a truly universal scale.

One way of defining temperature without reference to a specific material is to use a device called a constant-volume thermometer. A simplified sketch of such an apparatus is shown in Illustration 59. It is just a gas-filled container with rigid walls con-

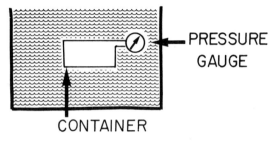

CONTAINER

Illustration 59

nected to a gauge that measures the pressure of the gas. The volume of the container doesn't change (that's what's meant by the term *constant volume*), so the pressure will be different if the thermometer is placed in different environments. For example, if we immerse the container in a bath of ice water at 32° F, we will get one pressure reading. If we then boil the water, the pressure will rise to a new value. The readings of the pressure gauge in these two situations will define the two ends of the Fahrenheit or Celsius scales, and the pressure reading in any other environment will give us a temperature in exactly the same way that the height of a column of mercury does.

Suppose that we had a tub of water whose temperature we wished to determine with a constant-volume thermometer. We would first immerse the device in a mixture of ice and water and read the pressure gauge. Call this reading the reference pressure. We would then remove the thermometer from that tub and put it into the tub whose temperature we want to know. A new pressure will show up on the gauge, and the ratio between this pressure and the reference pressure will depend on the difference in temperature between the two tubs. In this way we can convert the readings on the pressure gauge to degrees Fahrenheit or Celsius.

Unfortunately, there are complications involved in this procedure. Suppose for the sake of argument we had gone through the procedure just described with our thermometer filled with air. If we were to pump the air out of the container and replace it with oxygen, we could repeat the entire process. In a perfect world, we might expect to get the same pressure readings as before—the kind of gas in the thermometer wouldn't matter. In fact, we do not live in a perfect world, a point that has been made repeatedly by writers in other contexts. With oxygen instead of air in the thermometer, both the reference pressure and the final pressure (as well as the ratio between them) will be different. Using a third gas (for example, helium) would give us a third set of pressure readings different from the first two.

To make matters worse, even if we didn't replace the air in the original measurement with oxygen, but just pumped some of it out of the container, we still wouldn't reproduce the original set of pressure readings. In other words, not only does the change in pressure depend on the kind of material in the thermometer, it depends on how much material there is as well.

We could, of course, just go ahead and define a temperature scale in terms of a specified amount of a specified gas. For example, we might say that the readings given by a thermometer containing one pound of air are "right" and just calibrate all other thermometers accordingly. In effect, this is what we do when we talk about temperature in terms of an ordinary mercury thermometer. But this state of affairs bothers physicists. A fundamental quantity ought to have a fundamental definition and shouldn't depend on the kind of details we've been discussing.

That the readings on our thermometer change as the amount of gas is varied actually suggests a way to resolve this problem. Suppose we took a series of readings according to the procedure outlined above, and that between each set of measurements we extracted half of the gas that was in the container. Each set of measurements would differ slightly from the ones preceding it, of course. We can represent this difference by plotting the ratio of the pressure in the second tub to the reference pressure as a function of the amount of gas in the thermometer. If we did so, we'd get a series of points like those shown in Illustration 60. As the amount of gas decreases, the ratio between the measured and reference pressure drops slowly. We can imagine extrapolating these readings all the way to the left. The point where the extrapolation intersects the axis represents the expected result from a hypothetical experiment in which the temperature is measured by a thermometer containing no gas whatsoever!

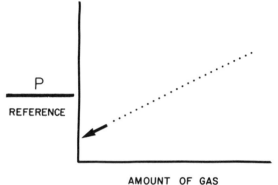

AMOUNT OF GAS

Illustration 60

If you think of the intersection as the limit of a set of readings in which the amount of gas in the thermometer is successively reduced, an important conclusion suggests itself. While it may be true that the temperature as measured by this thermometer depends on the type and amount of gas in the container, it is also reasonable to suppose that in the limit where the thermometer contains no gas, the particular type of gas that is being withdrawn, and is finally removed altogether, should not affect the position of the extrapolated "no-gas" point. In terms of Illustration 60, we expect that if we repeated the sequence of experiments for a thermometer containing different kinds of gases, they would all extrapolate to the same point on the vertical axis. In fact, this turns out to be the case. In Illustration 61 we show the results for several different kinds of gas.

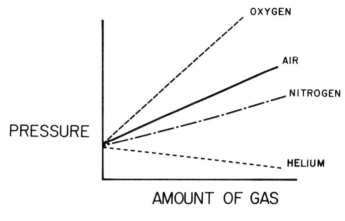

OXYGEN

AIR

NITROGEN

PRESSURE

HELIUM

AMOUNT OF GAS

Illustration 61

It appears, then, that after a fairly convoluted chain of reasoning and experimentation, we have found a number that can be related to temperature and that does not depend on the materials in the apparatus being used to make the measurements. The quantity we eventually derive from this operation is called the ideal gas temperature. And while the path to this new temperature scale has been complicated, there are several important lessons that can be learned from having traveled it.

First, it is clear that physicists are willing to go to enormous lengths to devise universal standards that are independent of measurement details. In part, such behavior is motivated by practical concerns; if you have something like the ideal gas temperature scale, then it really doesn't matter so much if the oxygen in your thermometer is slightly contaminated with nitrogen. You will still be able to compare results with people working in other laboratories. But by far the most important motivation is not practical, but aesthetic. It just *feels* wrong to have a temperature scale depend on the material in the thermometer, and I'm confident that physicists in the nineteenth century would have been just as avid in their pursuit of the ideal gas scale even if there were no practical advantages in such an achievement. The quest for universality is a major driving force in all areas of physics.

Second, the fact that it was so difficult to devise a suitable temperature scale is a reflection of the fact that we are still operating in the dark; we can define a way to measure temperature, but we really have no understanding of what it is. Until such time as we have such an understanding, it probably isn't too surprising that our attempts to deal with temperature will be a little clumsy.

Finally, once we have arrived at a universally accepted temperature scale, other new and interesting phenomena can be observed. For example, we can take a gas thermometer and go through the measuring scheme we've outlined for a succession of lower and lower temperature environments. Starting with steam, we could work down to boiling alcohol, then to dry ice, liquid nitrogen, and liquid helium. If we did so, and plotted the results, we would get a graph like Illustration 62. The ratio of pressures

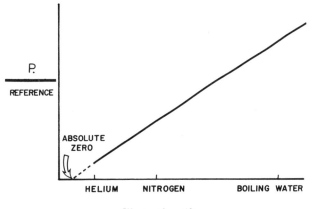

Illustration 62

in the zero-gas limit would fall as the temperature (measured in the conventional Fahrenheit or centigrade scale) fell. If we extended the straight line in the graph to temperatures below the freezing point of helium, the line so produced would quickly reach a value of the final pressure ratio equal to zero.

Pressure, by definition, is simply the force exerted on each square inch of the wall of the container by the gas. It's conceivable that the pressure of a gas could be zero, but it cannot be negative—such a number is simply meaningless. This means that the point at which the line in the graph crosses zero pressure represents the lowest possible temperature that can be attained. Any lower temperature would correspond to the impossible case of negative pressure. This temperature, which occurs at $-273.16°$C, has a special significance. It is called absolute zero and, although we shall see later that it has a simple interpretation in terms of molecular motion, it can be defined without any direct reference to atoms whatever. It is truly a fundamental quantity.

This means that absolute zero, unlike the freezing and boiling points of water, is *not* arbitrary if it is used to construct a temperature scale. The temperature scale used by scientists today, the so-called Kelvin scale, has the zero-degree point at absolute zero. Rather than define an arbitrary upper reference temperature, however, this scale simply defines the degree. One degree Kelvin (K) is defined to be exactly equal to one Celsius degree, and is therefore equal to ⅝ of a Fahrenheit degree.

Having now described how a temperature scale can be defined in theory, it might be a good idea to pause for a moment and ask how all of this is translated into practice. After all, in the normal course of industrial and scientific affairs one often wants to measure temperatures all the way from absolute zero to the melting point of metals. It would be very tedious to have to calibrate thermometers at the boiling and freezing points of water if they are to be used in much hotter or colder environments. Consequently, in 1968 the International Practical Temperature Scale was adopted. This scale defines a large number of reference temperatures that can easily be reproduced in the laboratory. The temperatures are defined in the Kelvin scale, and run all the way from the point at which hydrogen condenses into a liquid ($13.81°$K) to the melting point of gold ($1337.58°$K). In this way, one can calibrate a thermometer using reference temperatures near those at which it will actually be operating.

There is one more practical aspect of thermometry that we

have to discuss. The range of temperatures encountered in nature and in the laboratory is very large. In the list below we show some typical temperatures that might be found.

System	Temperature
Inside the sun	10^7
Solar surface	6000
Melting point of lead	600
Room temperature	300
Freezing point of water	273
Oxygen liquifies	90
Helium liquifies	4.2
Lowest temperature attained in the laboratory	10^{-6}

This wide range of temperatures actually requires a little more sophistication in the building of thermometers than we have discussed so far. For example, below $1°K$ the gas thermometer won't work well because gas pressures become too low to measure. In a similar fashion, if the temperature is high enough, any thermometer of the type we have described would melt.

Following the general scheme of finding properties of materials that depend on temperature and then using that property as a measure of temperature, we can devise several other types of thermometers.

The heat generated by an electrical current passing through a wire depends to some extent on the temperature of the wire. With proper calibration, this effect can be used to measure temperatures down to about $1°K$, below which point the sensitivity of this type of electrical resistance thermometer becomes poor. It has the advantage, however, that only a small coil of wire need be in the region whose temperature we wish to know, and measuring an electrical current is a simple operation compared to the complicated procedure needed to work a gas thermometer.

If we take wires made of two different metals and solder the ends together each to each as shown in Illustration 63, and then

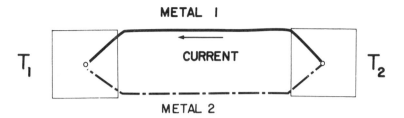

Illustration 63

put the two ends into different temperature environments, an electrical current will flow around the loop. The amount of current depends on the difference in temperature between the two ends, so if one end is kept (for example) in a container with melting ice and water, measuring this current will give a determination of the temperature of the other end. This device, called a thermocouple, has operating principles a little too complicated to go into here but is one of the most common temperature-measuring devices, because it is very simple to build. In addition, since its output is an electrical current, it is ideal for use in systems where computers are used to control temperatures. Thermocouples become difficult to use below about 50° K; therefore, they are seldom used to measure very low temperatures.

For temperatures below 1° K, the magnetic properties of matter can be utilized to make measurements. We know (see chapter 6) that in many atoms the movement of electrons in their orbits creates magnetic fields around the atom, and that for many purposes we can think of each atom as a tiny bar magnet with a north and a south pole. The movement of protons and neutrons inside the nucleus produces a similar (although smaller) effect. If a block of material is placed in a magnetic field, these little magnets will tend to align themselves with the field. The extent to which this alignment is successfully accomplished depends on the temperature of the material, and so can be used as an indication of temperature. Techniques using the alignment of atomic magnets can measure down to .001° K, while those using the smaller nuclear effects can go to temperatures a thousand times lower, to .000001°K.

At the other end of the temperature scale, we measure very high temperatures by measuring radiation, with an optical pyrometer. We know that if a piece of metal is heated it first becomes a dull red, then a bright red, and finally becomes white hot. In chapter 4 we saw that color is associated with the wavelength of electromagnetic radiation, and that this radiation exists in invisible as well as visible forms. We can measure the intensity of radiation emitted by an object at several wavelengths (for example, by viewing it first through a blue filter, then a red one). From this data, there are straightforward formulae that allow us to infer the object's temperature, just as our eyes can tell us that a red-hot object is cooler than one that is white hot.

Having established that it is possible to measure temperature and having discussed the way it is done, we can now turn our attention to the question we asked at the beginning—what is temperature? To answer this we have to make use of the fact that any material that has a temperature is made up of atoms, and that any property of that material can be related in some way to the behavior of atoms.

Take pressure as an example. When we inflate a tire, we have some sense that the air is exerting a force on the walls of the tire and is thus supporting the weight of the car. In fact, we can define pressure as the force exerted by the air divided by the surface area of the tire (the area of the inner tube). This would be a macroscopic definition, one that does not depend on atoms.

If, however, we were able to look at the wall of the tire with a kind of supermicroscope, we would see air molecules bouncing off of it constantly. Each time a molecule bounces, it exerts a force on the wall, and the total effect of all these collisions is what we perceive as pressure. This sort of microscopic description of the pressure would not involve large-scale forces and areas, but would instead take account of the masses and velocities of the molecules and the frequency with which the molecules bounce off the wall.

Clearly, these two descriptions of pressure are complementary. They simply represent two ways of looking at the same thing. One, the macroscopic, involves large-scale quantities that we can detect with our senses. The other, the microscopic, deals with the properties of atoms that we cannot see directly. From an experimental point of view, it is much easier to contrive a macroscopic definition of any quantity. That is why this sort of explanation came first in the history of science. Yet there is no denying that describing phenomena in terms of atomic motion is more satisfying because it is more basic.

Our discussion of temperature is a good case in point. We have gone to great lengths to define quantities like absolute zero completely in terms of macroscopic measurements. There has been no use as yet of the concept of the atom, and this restraint in our discussion makes it a good paradigm of the development of the concept of temperature. But though we have come quite far, we still haven't really said what temperature is. We've managed to talk our way around the question. The root of the trouble is that we have not yet provided a microscopic definition of temperature.

If we consider our example of pressure, we see that we need three things to provide a complete description of a phenomenon. We need the microscopic and macroscopic pictures, of course, and then we need a statement that connects the two, what philosophers call a bridge statement. In the case of pressure, the bridge statement would be something like "The force you calculate from the molecular collisions is the same force you measure with a tire gauge."

This statement may seem trivial; actually it touches on a very deep philosophical matter, the question of the relationship between the physical world and the ideas about the world that exist in our minds. In the late nineteenth century, no one had ever seen an atom. All the evidence for the existence of atoms was indirect. People believed in atoms because they provided a simple and elegant explanation for many physical effects, but they would have been forced to admit that the existence of such effects in the world could not be proved. Thus, the division between microscopic and macroscopic descriptions in science calls to mind in a more difficult form the very old philosophical distinction between object and thought. The quest for a satisfying definition of temperature, then, comes to nothing less than a demand that we find a way to bridge the gap between these two.

The development of a microscopic definition of temperature is a little more involved than what we have just outlined for pressure, but it follows the same general pattern. We have seen that the Kelvin temperature scale can be defined in terms of the pressure registered by a gas in a gas thermometer. If we use the microscopic description of pressure to describe this gas, a little mathematics leads us to the following equation:

$$\tfrac{1}{2}mv^2 = \tfrac{3}{2}kT$$

On the left-hand side of this equation we have one-half the mass of a single molecule of gas multiplied by the square of the average velocity of the molecules. On the right we have the ordinary Kelvin temperature, T, multiplied by a number, k, known as Boltzmann's constant (after Ludwig Boltzmann, the Austrian physicist who first discovered this relation).

The equation has a simple interpretation. It tells us that what we perceive and measure as temperature is related to the energy contained in the motion of molecules. The faster the molecules move, the higher the temperature. The consequences of this idea are discussed in chapter 1, but for the moment we simply note that this interpretation of the equation gives us a much more satisfying picture of temperature than anything we have encountered so far. Even the concept of absolute zero can be easily interpreted, because we see that $T = 0$ in the Boltzmann equation corresponds to the case of nonmoving molecules ($v = 0$). In other words, as the velocity of the gas molecules falls, so does the temperature we measure. But the velocity of a molecule cannot be less than zero, for once you are standing still you can't move any more slowly. At this point the temperature is as low as it can possibly be. (Technically, quantum mechanics tells us that the lowest velocity a molecule can have is not zero, but a small positive number called the zero-point velocity.)

This atomic description of temperature is more intellectually satisfying than the definition in terms of the ideal gas scale, since it provides a picture that is easy to visualize. Higher temperatures simply correspond to atoms zipping around faster. But at a deeper level it is a truly remarkable result, because it shows, in a strict mathematical sense, exactly what the relation between a macroscopic quantity (temperature) and a microscopic one (atomic velocity) is. It provides the bridge between the world and our conceptual schemes about it, and as such rightly enjoys a central place in discussions of the philosophy of science.

It appears that thinking about an everyday concept like temperature has led us to nothing less than the missing link between atoms and ourselves.

8

Why Does Hot Air Come Out of the Bottom of a Refrigerator Even Though the Inside Is Cold?

ILLUSTRATION 64 SHOWS THE ESSENTIAL WORKING PARTS OF THE kind of refrigerator you probably have in your kitchen. At point *A* a liquid (usually Freon refrigerants) under high pressure squirts through a nozzle into a pipe. The boiling point of the liquid at normal pressure is about 40° F, so once it's in the pipe it begins to evaporate, pulling heat from its surroundings to do so. Anything that happens to be near the evaporating Freon refrigerants (for example, a tomato in the refrigerator) is cooled.

The Freon vapor then goes to a motor-driven compressor where it is subjected to a high pressure. This converts vapor back into a liquid, heating it even more in the process. The hot liquid is then run into a series of thin pipes (this is the black grid at the back of your refrigerator). Here the heat is absorbed by the air. The cooled liquid goes back to the nozzle to start the process again,

121

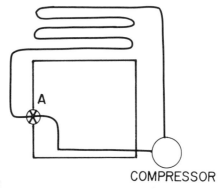

Illustration 64

COMPRESSOR

while the heated air is forced out so that you feel it when you put your hand under the refrigerator.

The refrigerator, then, is simply a device that absorbs heat in a working fluid and then transfers that heat to the air. Incidentally, if the vapor expansion valve and cooling coil were located outside a house, either in the ground or in the air, and the heat was released inside the house, then we would have a heat pump, a device that has become familiar in this energy-conscious age as an efficient means of heating a home.

To a physicist, the refrigerator is just one example of a machine that operates between environments that are at two different temperatures. A physicist's view of the refrigerator is shown in Illustration 65. There is one heat reservoir at a high tempera-

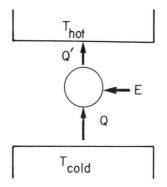

Illustration 65

ture, T_{hot}, and another at a low temperature, T_{cold}. For an ordinary refrigerator these are the outside air and the things being cooled, respectively. An amount of heat, customarily labeled by the letter Q, is removed from the cold reservoir, and an amount Q' is deposited in the warm one. To accomplish all this, an amount of energy E is needed—energy that comes from the electric company. This energy is needed to run the compressor and move the Freon refrigerants around. Since all the heat that is taken from the cold reservoir eventually finds its way to the hot one, there is no loss of energy in the system. There is one aspect of the behavior of a refrigerator, however, that is so obvious we tend to overlook it. *The refrigerator will not work unless it is plugged in.*

This is a special case of a rule that physicists call the Second Law of Thermodynamics. Like most profound statements, it is so obvious that your first reaction on seeing it is to say, "Of course. How could it be otherwise?" Yet the implications of this statement touch every aspect of our lives and even provide us with a preview of what the end of the universe will be like. The general statement of the law is:

> Heat will not flow from a cold to a hot object spontaneously.

Perhaps an example will make the reasonableness of this statement clear. If you put an ice cube in your sink, heat from the surrounding air (a warm object) will flow into the ice cube (a cold object). The net effect is that the ice cube eventually melts and the resulting water comes to room temperature. If we should see heat flowing from the ice cube into the air—in other words, see the air warming up and the ice cube getting colder—then the law as we have stated it would be violated.

The revolutionary aspect of this seemingly innocuous statement about everyday experience can be appreciated best by thinking about the First Law of Thermodynamics. In chapter 1 we saw the heat extracted from the contents of the refrigerator, the mechanical work done by the compressor, the electrical energy used by the system, and the chemical energy in the fuel burned by the power plant to generate that electricity are all interchangeable. According to the law, transferring a given amount of heat from the ice cube to the air and from the air to the ice cube are both perfectly equivalent and reversible processes. The point to note is that the energy can't just disappear—it has to be conserved. But what the ice cube example also shows is that there is something more to the energy story. While it is *possible* for the ice cube to get colder and colder while it sits in the sink, in point of fact it does not. There seems to be something operating in nature that gives a direction to heat flow.

This statement of the Second Law of Thermodynamics seems so general that it might appear at first that it would be impossible to draw any important conclusions from it. In fact, we can use this statement to deduce an important property of engines. We can prove that it is impossible to construct an engine that has no other effect than to extract a certain amount of energy in the form of heat from a hot object and convert that energy completely into mechanical work. The proof of this statement is so simple that we can go through the argument ourselves. Suppose such an engine were possible. Then in our physicist's view of things, it would look like the device in Illustration 66. It would remove an amount of

Illustration 66

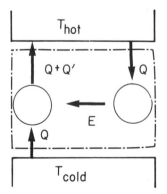

heat Q' from a reservoir at T_{hot} and convert it into an equivalent amount of work E without dumping any waste heat into the cold reservoir.

But if this were possible, then we could use the energy produced by the hypothetical machine to run an ordinary refrigerator. This refrigerator would remove an amount of heat Q from the cold reservoir and return this amount plus the energy E to the hot reservoir. But if we consider the hypothetical engine and the refrigerator to be a single engine (imagine that the two are housed in a single box indicated by the dashed line), then this combined engine would remove an amount of heat Q from the cold reservoir and deposit a net amount of heat Q in the hot reservoir without using any work at all. In other words, the combined machine would cause heat to flow spontaneously from a cold to a hot body!

Since we know such a spontaneous flow does not occur (for the same reason that we know a refrigerator won't work unless it's plugged in), we can conclude that the engine that completely converts heat into work can't exist.

These two statements—that heat will not go from a cold to a hot body and that heat cannot be completely converted to work—are so closely intertwined that they are generally regarded as equivalent statements of the Second Law of Thermodynamics. They establish the important limitations that nature puts on the interchangeability of heat with other forms of energy. In effect, they say that if you want to get a job done by producing a high temperature (for example, by burning gasoline in your car), then you *must* eject some of the energy in the burning fuel into the environment as waste heat. To claim otherwise is logically equivalent to saying it is possible to build a refrigerator that will run without being plugged in.

This requirement also means that once the waste heat has been deposited in the lowest temperature reservoir in the environment, it can no longer be turned into useful work. In practice, this usually means that once waste heat has been dumped into the atmosphere or the ocean, it becomes unavailable for running an engine. For example, there is as much energy in the motion of the molecules in a cubic mile of sea water as there is in a year's output of more than one hundred electrical generating plants. What the Second Law tells us is that even though this energy is there, we can't use it.

This constraint is particularly important to modern industrial societies because so much of the energy we use comes from creating hot "reservoirs" by burning fossil fuels. Whether it's gasoline in an automobile or coal in a power plant, there is almost always a high-temperature process underlying the machines that run our society. You might characterize the entire energy economy of a modern industrial state as a device for taking chemical energy stored in hydrocarbons and exhausting waste heat into the environment. In the process we eventually convert the available energy in the fuel to unavailable energy in the form of low-grade heat. So, as we burn up our coal and oil, we are consuming the easily available forms of energy, forcing future generations to find alternative (and more difficult) ways of producing their hot reservoirs.

Given the amount of work we get from heat-driven engines today, it's hard to realize that only two centuries ago the main source of motive power was muscle—either human or animal. The early eighteenth century was an exciting time, because just as the need for a new source of power became pressing, a small group of engineers began to discover how to tap the enormous energy stored underground in the form of coal. Before then, the only use for any kind of hydrocarbon fuel was as a direct source of heat. With the development of the steam engine by Thomas Newcomen and James Watt in the years before the American Revolution, it became possible to use the heat generated by burning coal to do work—to run factories, ships, and locomotives. The great conversion of stored energy into waste heat had begun, and the world has never been the same.

But even though commercial heat engines had been on the market for several decades before 1800, there was no real scientific understanding of the laws that made them work. The development of the science of heat, and particularly of heat engines, was done by a young French engineer by the name of Sadi Carnot. Son of one of Napoleon's generals and an artillery officer himself, Carnot was concerned that almost all the development of the new steam engines was being done in England. He understood the dangers this posed to France and, as one of the first generation of young Frenchmen to be educated at the new École Polytechnique in Paris (an institution founded by Napoleon to train engineers and still the most prestigious technical school in France), he set out to understand the workings of the heat engine on a scientific basis.

Despite frequent interruptions for service in the Napoleonic wars, Carnot published a monograph in 1819 that contained, along with a number of studies relating to the workings of the steam engine, an accurate statement of the Second Law of Thermodynamics. Carnot was the first scientist to approach the problem of the heat engine from the point of view of the physicist, that is, the first to ask about the behavior of an abstract ideal of an engine, rather than about how to improve a model that was already in production. This line of inquiry led him to a consequence of the Second Law that has enormous import for the modern debate about energy policy.

Carnot began by trying to imagine the simplest possible device that had all the essential features of a real steam engine. The result of his thought was an idealized, frictionless machine (now known as the Carnot engine). It is pictured in Illustration 67.

In essence, the Carnot engine consists of a gas-filled cylinder that can be brought into contact with two reservoirs—one at a temperature T_{hot} and the other at a temperature T_{cold}. The first step in the engine's operation is shown in Illustration 67a. The cylinder is brought into contact with the hot reservoir, and an amount of heat, which we'll call Q_{hot}, flows into the gas. This causes the gas to expand, pushing the piston up. If there is a weight on the piston as shown, then the expanding gas does work by lifting the weight. You can think of this phase of the Carnot cycle as being analogous to the power stroke in an automobile engine, when the piston is pushed down by the ignition of the gasoline and the resulting motion is used to move the car.

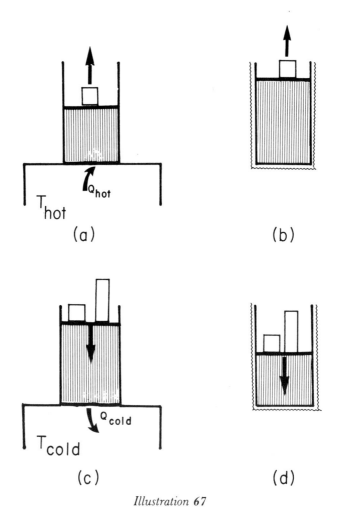

Illustration 67

The next phase of the Carnot cycle, shown in Illustration 67b, consists of isolating the cylinder from any heat source (think of wrapping it in very good insulation). Since the gas is hot, it will continue to expand, lifting the weight and doing more work in the process. Since there is no heat source to draw on, however, the expanding gas will cool off. This phase of operation continues until the gas temperature reaches T_{cold}, the temperature of the cold reservoir.

At this point, we have gotten all of the work out of the expanding gas that we can. In order to have a real engine, we now have to return the gas to its original state so that the cycle can start again. This will require work on our part. One way for us to perform this work is to lift a weight up to the new position of the piston. If we do this, and at the same time put the cylinder in contact with the cold reservoir (see Illustration 67c), then the added weight will force the piston down, compressing the gas. Ordinarily the temperature of the gas would rise at this point, just as an air pump gets warm when you blow up a bicycle tire. If the compression is done slowly, however, the heat that would go to warming the gas can flow into the cold reservoir, and the gas temperature will remain constant. The amount of heat that flows into the cold reservoir can be called Q_{cold}. This is what we have been calling "waste heat" up to this point. We see in this example that the appearance of waste heat is intimately connected to the need to return an engine to its original state after work has been done— to the requirement, in other words, that the engine run on a cycle. The two insulated parts of the cycle act to change the temperature of the gas between that of the hot reservoir and that of the cold reservoir.

The final stage of the Carnot process involves insulating the cylinder once more. Without the cold reservoir to accept the waste heat, the gas temperature will increase as the weight presses down. If we choose the weight carefully, the gas pressure will just balance it when the gas temperature reaches T_{hot}. At this point we can remove the weight we added after the second step in the cycle, put the cylinder back into contact with the hot reservoir, and begin the whole thing again.

The analogy between the Carnot engine and a real heat engine, like the one in your car, should be obvious. What we have been calling the hot reservoir is just the heat that is generated by burning hydrocarbons. In your car, you could think of this reservoir as the burning gasoline-air mixture in the cylinder. The cold reservoir is the ambient air into which the engine heat is exhausted. The work done by the expanding gas is what moves the car forward, and work done by the weight in compressing the gas corresponds to the work done in putting the piston back to the top of the cylinder in the car. A similar analogy could be drawn between the Carnot engine and any other device that produces work from a burning fuel.

Like any ideal, a real Carnot engine would be impossible to build, if for no other reason than that it takes no account of friction between its moving parts. Nevertheless, by thinking about it, Carnot was able to come to four very important conclusions.

First, the Carnot engine delivers a net amount of work. If you take the amount of work necessary to lift the additional weight up to the piston after step b, shown in Illustration 67, and subtract it from the work done by the expanding gas in steps a and b, the result is positive. Each time the engine proceeds around the cycle a net amount of useful work is done.

Second, there is no engine operating between reservoirs at T_{hot} and T_{cold} that is more efficient than the Carnot engine. This statement is not obvious but the proof is very similar to the proof that every engine must generate waste heat. The idea is to assume the opposite of what you want to prove, and then show that this assumption is equivalent to having a refrigerator that runs without being plugged in. If we assume that there is an engine more efficient than the Carnot engine, we can use that engine to run a refrigerator. A chain of argument somewhat more complicated than the one we used earlier shows that the existence of such a machine would imply the existence of a machine that transferred heat from a cold to a hot object without requiring any input energy.

Third, the efficiency of a Carnot engine is given by

$$\eta = 1 - \frac{T_{cold}}{T_{hot}}$$

where T_{hot} and T_{cold} are measured in the Kelvin scale (see chapter 7). The efficiency of any device is usually defined as the work you get out of it divided by the energy you put in. For the Carnot cycle, the burning of the fuel supplies an amount of energy Q_{hot} to the system, while a net amount of work is done by the moving piston, as discussed above. The ratio between these two numbers is the efficiency of the engine, and Carnot showed it was related to the temperatures of the two reservoirs by the above formula. This is an extremely important result, since it tells us the maximum efficiency *any* engine will have if operated between the same two temperatures. Some practical examples using this formula are given below.

Fourth, in a Carnot engine the quantity $Q_{hot}/T_{hot} - Q_{cold}/T_{cold}$ is zero. For any real engine it is greater than zero. The heat absorbed or given off by a substance divided by the temperature of the substance is called the change in entropy of the substance. While this definition may seem a bit formal and arbitrary, entropy can be visualized easily in terms of atomic motion, as we shall see. In the Carnot cycle, the first term in the expression is the change in entropy during phase a shown in Illustration 67, when heat is being added to the gas. The second term is the entropy change when heat is exhausted to the cold reservoir in phase c, the minus sign signifying the fact that heat is leaving, rather than entering, the gas. Hence, this statement says that the net change in entropy in the Carnot cycle is zero, but that any real engine will always have a net positive entropy change—a net increase in entropy— each time it goes around.

Actually, conclusions three and four aren't independent of each other. If we make a schema of the Carnot engine, as in Illustration 68, then conservation of energy requires that E, the net

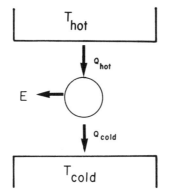

Illustration 68

amount of work done, be given by $Q_{hot} - Q_{cold}$, the difference between the heat taken in and the heat exhausted. Since efficiency is defined as W/Q_{hot} it follows from conclusion four that

$$\eta = \frac{W}{Q_{hot}} = \frac{Q_{hot} - Q_{cold}}{Q_{hot}} = 1 - \frac{Q_{cold}}{Q_{hot}} = 1 - \frac{T_{cold}}{T_{hot}}$$

which is just conclusion three.

The limitation on the efficiency of an engine is probably one of the most important statements that thermodynamics has to make about energy policy. Aside from the growing shortage of liquid hydrocarbons, few things produce more debate than the question of how to generate electricity. Given the fact that one solution to the gasoline shortage is the design of an electric car, this debate can only become more heated in the future.

An electrical generator is a device that takes heat created by some process, such as the burning of coal or the fissioning of uranium, and converts it into work by spinning the shaft of a turbine, which, in turn, converts this rotational energy into electricity. The process of converting the heat energy into rotation is one specific example of producing work from heat and must therefore be subject to the Second Law. From the discussion of the Carnot cycle, we know that the maximum efficiency that a generator can have is the efficiency of a Carnot engine operating between a hot reservoir at the temperature of the steam and a cold reservoir at the temperature of the surrounding air. For a steam engine operating at normal pressure, the temperature of the steam will be 100°C (212°F) or 373°K. If the outside air is at 300°K (about 70°F or 27°C), the maximum efficiency of such a device will be only 20 percent—fully four-fifths of the energy in the coal will be converted to unavailable waste heat.

The only way to counteract this low efficiency is to raise the temperature (and therefore the pressure) of the steam. In a modern generating plant steam may be used at 500°K. The maximum possible efficiency of a modern plant, then, will be about 40 percent. To go to still higher temperatures would require pressures and temperatures that no available pipe could withstand.

In point of fact, electrical engineers have pushed the efficiency ratings of modern generating plants into the 30 to 35 percent range, almost to the Carnot limit itself. There is no way they can do better without violating the Second Law—in effect, without building a refrigerator that will run without being plugged in.

So energy policymakers find themselves on the horns of a dilemma. On the one hand, the demand for electricity is going up, but on the other, the laws of nature require that for every kilowatt-hour of electricity we produce, two kilowatt-hours of the fuel's energy is dumped as waste heat. This has led some to write of adopting a "soft" energy path, one in which electricity is used only for those jobs (such as lighting and running motors) for which it is essential. Other present-day uses of electricity, such as water and space heating, would be handled by solar energy. Whether such a course is economically or even technically feasible is a subject of debate right now, but the basic reason for the existence of the debate is the limit expressed in the law of thermodynamics.

Another scheme based on the inevitability of producing waste heat when electricity is generated is called cogeneration. This has been tried with some success in Europe. The basic idea is to build industrial plants right next to generating stations and to use the waste heat produced by the generator to supply industrial steam (or other kinds of industrial heat) to the factories. In this way, the waste heat isn't really wasted.

Important as these considerations are, the most interesting applications of the Second Law have to do with the long-range future of the universe. The easiest way to discuss this aspect of the law is to refer to the concept of entropy. When we talked about the Carnot engine, we introduced this quantity by saying that the change in entropy of a system was equal to the heat that went into the system divided by the temperature of the system while the heat was being added. This definition, although correct, can hardly be said to give us any insight into the meaning of the term.

We can get a much better feeling for entropy by thinking

about atoms. When we look at anything, what we see are macro-scopic things—size, temperature, pressure, and so on. We know that what we see is somehow related to what the atoms or mole-cules are doing in the object, but we don't actually *see* atoms. Take pressure as an example. We know that when we blow up a bal-loon or pump up a tire, there is an increase in the force that the molecules exert on the container walls. If we could look at the inside wall with high magnification, we would see something like the situation pictured on the left in Illustration 69. Fast-moving

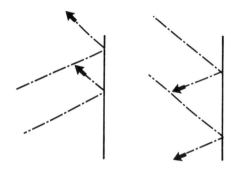

Illustration 69

molecules strike the wall and rebound. Each such collision causes a small force to be exerted, and the pressure we see is just the aggregate of all of the forces exerted by all the molecules.

The point in this connection between a macroscopic quantity (pressure) and microscopic events is this: we can measure only the former and have no way of determining the latter. For example, if the directions of the molecules in the figure on the left in Illus-tration 69 were reversed, giving rise to the figure on the right, there would be no change in pressure. The net result of the two collisions would be the same for either situation, and there is no way that we can tell which actually occurred just by looking at the pressure. In fact, when you realize that there are roughly 10^{26}

molecules in a few grams of material, you can see that there will be a large number of ways in which the molecules could be shuffled around without changing the readings on any of our instruments. In a sense, molecular motion represents a sort of giant shell game in which the external, perceived reality is the same for many different arrangements of the interior structure.

The number of ways a system can be internally rearranged without changing the macroscopic data is called the statistical weight of the system. A system with high statistical weight is one that can switch back and forth between a large number of configurations without our being able to detect any change. Such a system is said to have a high level of disorder.

In the late nineteenth century, the concept of disorder was used to define a new sort of entropy. In effect, the new entropy was a mathematical function of the statistical weight of a system. One of the great triumphs of that generation of physicists was to show that this new kind of entropy, which is the measure of the disorder of a system, and the old kind, defined in terms of heat and temperature, were exactly the same. Although the general proof requires some mathematics, we can give a simple argument to show why this conclusion is reasonable. From our discussion in chapter 1, we know that if we add heat to a system the atoms in the system will, on the average, move faster. This means that a heated system has more states available to the atoms than does the corresponding unheated system, since in the former case a given atom can move with a wider variety of velocities. To use our analogy, adding heat increases the number of shells in the great shell game. This means that the statistical weight increases when heat is added to a system and, hence, that the disorder increases.

In this language, the Second Law says that in any cyclical process the entropy of the system must increase or, at best, stay constant. It cannot decrease. The universe, in other words, must always evolve in the direction of increasing entropy. If we follow this line of thinking to its logical conclusion, we expect that eventually the universe must wind up as a vast featureless blob of totally disordered matter. This is called the ultimate heat death of the universe.

Although the Second Law does seem to imply this ultimate future for us, it says nothing about the exact process by which heat death will be achieved. There is a certain morose pleasure in thinking about this question; in fact, a fairly good picture of what the ultimate fate of the universe will be can be gleaned from our present knowledge of physical laws.

In our own neighborhood, we know that the sun will run out of nuclear fuel in about 5 billion years (5×10^9 years in scientific notation). At that point it will start to cool and expand, becoming a type of star known as a red giant. Its outer periphery will probably be outside the earth's orbit, so our own planet will be absorbed. Later, the sun will shrink down to a white dwarf and, in 100 billion years or so, will become just a burned-out cinder floating in space. A similar fate awaits most of the stars that are like the sun. For reference, the universe is now only about 15 billion years old, so we are talking about a time in the future ten times the total age of the universe.

Larger stars will have a more spectacular ending, exploding as supernovae and collapsing down to neutron stars or into black holes. At this point things start to slow down. The leisurely time scale involved in the burning out of the stars is replaced by a still more leisurely time scale, as the remnants of the galaxy move around and collide with one another. In a time scale of 10^{28} years, the cinders and small stars can be expected to encounter black holes. When this happens the cinders will be torn apart and will stream into the black hole, never to emerge again. As this collision process goes on, all the matter in the galaxy will eventually wind up inside the black holes.

But that's not the end. During all this time the expansion of the universe will be continuing. Eventually, the temperature of the background radiation will be less than the temperature of the black holes, and a new process will start. According to the laws of quantum mechanics, the black holes will begin to radiate energy into space. In essence, they start to evaporate, dumping their energy into the radiation bath around them. This process takes about 10^{53} years for a solar-size black hole. When it is over, there will be nothing left anywhere except an endless expanding sea of photons and neutrinos. The Second Law of Thermodynamics will have won its last battle.

Perhaps it was contemplating this scenario that caused 1979 Nobel laureate Steven Weinberg to remark, "The more the universe becomes comprehensible, the more it also seems pointless."

9

Lessons from a Light Bulb

WHEN THOMAS EDISON INVENTED THE ORDINARY INCANDESCENT light bulb, he was looking for a clean lighting system to replace the gas lanterns and oil lamps prevalent in his day. He succeeded in his quest, as we all know, but from the point of view of energy, the electric light bulb is not primarily a lighting system. An ordinary 100-watt bulb, for example, will produce about 5 watts of visible light and 95 watts of heat in the form of infrared radiation. In a sense, Edison's invention is nothing more than a device for taking expensive energy in the form of electricity and turning it into low-grade energy in the form of heat, producing a little light as a byproduct.

The heat a light bulb can emit is well known to those who have to deal with plumbing in cold weather. A standard country remedy for preventing the freezing of water pipes is to leave a light bulb burning in the basement overnight. The heat provided by the bulb is often enough to keep the water flowing. One-hundred-watt bulbs are also used to heat incubators for newly hatched chicks and to carry out countless other jobs in which a cheap, low-intensity heat source is needed. So, although our primary perception of the bulb is as a source of light, its utility as a heater has not gone entirely unnoticed.

Our question, then, is how an electrical current in a bulb gives rise to so much heat and so little light. To answer the question, we first have to understand exactly what an electric current is and how it transfers energy to the bulb in the first place.

We have learned that a single atom contains two kinds of electrical charges, the positive charge in the heavy nucleus and the negative charge in the electrons in orbit. In general, each isolated atom has as much negative charge in its electrons as it has positive charge in its nucleus, so that the overall effect is of an object with no electrical charge at all. When atoms come together to form ordinary materials, this electrical neutrality may or may not be preserved. In some materials, like common table salt (sodium chloride), some atoms give up electrons, becoming positively charged in the process, and other atons pick up the electrons, becoming negatively charged. Atoms in which the charges on the electrons do not cancel the charge of the nucleus are called ions. For the material as a whole, the net electrical charge is still zero, but each atom is no longer electrically neutral, since it has either one too many or one too few electrons.

In the metals that we normally think of as being used to carry electrical current—copper or aluminum, for example—a somewhat different situation exists. Here each atom of the metal loses one or more electrons, but there are no atoms around to pick these electrons up. The result is shown in Illustration 70. The metal consists of an array of positive ions (i.e., metal atoms that have lost electrons), and around these ions float a veritable sea of free electrons. These electrons were given up by the atoms when the metal was formed, but they have long since ceased to retain any attachment to their place of origin. In a very real sense, these electrons belong to the entire metal, rather than to any single atom. They

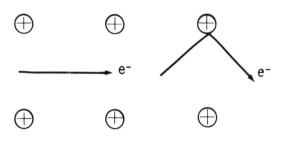

Illustration 70

normally move quite rapidly and hence are not trapped when they approach the positive ions, even though there is an attractive force between the two. In this sense, they are like cars on a highway: they are not held back by small holes or surface depressions because they are moving fast enough to go right on through.

A material in which electrons are free to move like this is called a conductor. If we apply a force to the free electrons, they will move in the direction of the force. We call the resulting flow of charged particles an electrical current. You can, in fact, think of the flow of electrons in a wire as being analogous to the flow of cars along a highway. If you were asked about the traffic flow on a road, one way to answer the question would be to stand by the side of the road and count the number of cars going by. You might find, for example, that there was a flow of 100 cars per hour, or perhaps 3 cars per minute.

In the same way, if you could imagine a microscopic traffic engineer standing next to a wire and counting electrons, he could tell us how many electrons per second were going by his post. If he counted 6.3×10^{18} electrons going by each second, he would say that there was a current of one amp (amp being an abbreviation of Ampère, the unit named after André Ampère, one of the pioneers of the science of electricity).

For the sake of completeness, we should point out that not

every material has free electrons in it. When atoms form to combine some types of material (for example, wax or plastic), every electron is firmly attached. In this case, applying a force will not cause any electrons to move through the material simply because there are no electrons free to do so. Such a material is called an insulator. Finally, there are a few materials, most notably the minerals silicon and germanium, in which electrons are locked in as in an insulator, but are locked in very loosely. Even the relatively mild motions associated with atomic motion at room temperature are enough to shake a few electrons loose. Such materials will conduct electricity, but will do so much less easily than a metal like copper. They are called semiconductors, and form the basis of the so-called solid-state industry in the United States. Which of these three possible properties a given material will have with respect to the flow of electrons depends on the structure of the individual atoms involved. The general principle is that the electrons in each material will arrange themselves in a way that minimizes the total energy of the solid (see chapter 3).

In a conductor, then, some electrons find themselves free to move within a matrix of heavy positive ions. When a current is flowing in the wire, we would expect to see a situation like the one in Illustration 71. Electrons will be accelerated and pick up speed as they go. When they encounter one of the heavy ions, however, they will rebound, much as a Ping-Pong ball would rebound if it hit a large boulder in its path. These collisions prevent the electrons from achieving too great a velocity in the wire, of course, but they have another effect as well. In each collision between an electron and an ion, the ion gains a little energy and moves a little faster. Since the ion is effectively anchored by the metallic structure, this increased velocity manifests itself as a more rapid vibration of the ion in the metallic framework. If you picture the metal as a sort of Tinkertoy arrangement, with the ions representing the pieces where the struts join together, then this motion can be pictured as a small vibration of these pieces around their normal position. The net effect of the movement of the electrical current is to cause this vibrational activity to increase.

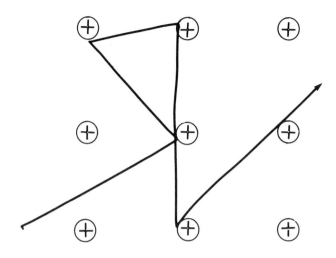

Illustration 71

In chapter 1, we saw that atomic vibration is directly related to what we perceive to be the temperature of the material of which the atoms are composed. The faster the atoms move, the higher the temperature. For a piece of wire with an electrical current running through it, we expect that the inevitable collisions between the electrons and the ions will cause the ions to vibrate more rapidly, thereby increasing the temperature of the metal. Therefore, the answer to the question we began with is that a light bulb gets hot because the electrons that make up the current flowing through it collide with ions in the metal wire and make them move faster.

The property of a metal that causes the energy of motion of the electrons to be converted to heat is called electrical resistance. In some metals the spacing and binding of the ions is such that it is relatively easy for them to absorb energy from the electron stream. Such metals are said to have a high resistance, since they produce a relatively large amount of heat from the electrical current. The tungsten filament in a light bulb is this sort of material, since when you turn on the switch it attains a temperature at which it glows white hot. The material in the heating coil of your toaster also has a high resistance, as you can easily deduce from the fact that it glows red in the process of making your breakfast. In general, whenever we want to produce heat from electricity, as we do in the toaster and household heating systems, we use a very high-resistance material to make sure that the maximum amount of the energy carried in the flow of electrons is converted into heat.

There are many situations, however, in which we want to do just the opposite—minimize the heat generated by the current. When we want to move electrical energy from one point to another—from power station to town, for example, or from the power lines to the light bulb in our home—we do not want to waste energy by generating a lot of heat. A material that has relatively little energy transfer in electron-ion collisions would be in order here; we say that such materials have a low electrical resistance. The most common low-resistance materials are copper and aluminum, although gold and silver are occasionally used in special circumstances (such as spacecraft) where cost is not important.

Thus, even in such a mundane job as household electrical wiring, the details of the atomic collision process between moving electrons and heavy ions in a metal wire plays an important role. Most people are surprised at how many such collisions there are even in a good conductor like copper. The motion of an electron through a wire is much more like a running back smashing into a swarm of tacklers than a sprinter streaking unobstructed down the track. In any collision an electron is almost as likely to bounce back from the ion as it is to emerge moving forward. An electron path might look something like Illustration 72. The overall motion is a seemingly random set of changes in direction upon which is imposed a slow drift in the direction of the current. In the wires leading to your 100-watt bulb, this drift velocity is quite small. On the average, the progress of a single electron will be measured in fractions of an inch per second, a good deal slower than the speed of walking.

During the late nineteenth century, when the first public

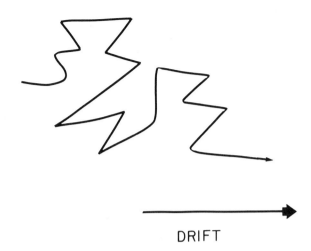

DRIFT

Illustration 72

power plants were being built and electricity was starting to change everybody's lives, scientists were very much interested in understanding the laws of electrical resistance. They developed the general picture outlined here, but went further. They began to ask how various factors, including temperature, affected the resistance of a conductor. Surprisingly enough, this investigation, seemingly of interest only to a handful of professional physicists, led to a discovery that may well affect the lives of everyone living in advanced societies in the next few decades.

From the point of view of an electron, a conducting wire might look something like the situation on the left in Illustration 73. If we look down the wire on a microscopic level we see the matrix of heavy ions in front of us. Because the wire is at a normal temperature, these ions will be vibrating around their equilibrium points. The effect of this vibration is to "smear out" each ion, so that the probability of the electron getting through without hitting an ion is considerably diminished.

If we lower the temperature of the wire, however, the situation begins to look like that pictured on the right in Illustration

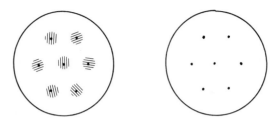

Illustration 73

73. The vibration of the ions decreases, and consequently the smeared-out area decreases as well. The effect of this "shrinking" is to open up more space for the electrons to move through, thereby decreasing the number of collisions. Since it is these collisions that give rise to resistance, we would expect that as the temperature of a wire is lowered, its electrical resistance (and the heat generated by passing a current through it) will decrease. At very low temperatures resistance should become very small.

In 1911 the Dutch physicist Heike Kamerlingh Onnes, working in Leiden, was measuring the resistance of a small cylinder of mercury at very low temperatures, seeking to verify this prediction. As he lowered the temperature, he saw the resistance of his sample decreasing smoothly. Then, at a temperature of about −269°C (−452°F, just 4.2° above the absolute zero discussed in chapter 7), the resistance dropped to zero. Not just to a small number, mind you, but completely to zero.

From what was known about the atomic origin of resistance, this result was completely unexplainable. So long as the electrons move through the wire, they must collide with ions. These collisions must make the ions move more rapidly, and the current must therefore generate heat. It's hard to see how changing the temperature by a fraction of a degree could do anything to affect such a fundamental process.

The phenomenon that Onnes discovered by accident is called superconductivity. It occurs in a variety of metals other than mer-

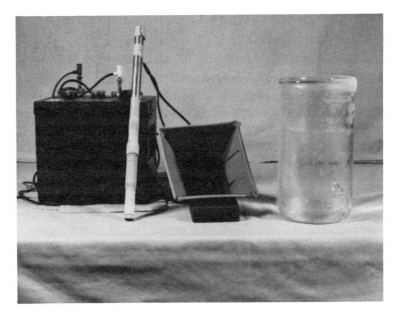

Current from a battery runs through a coil of ordinary copper wire wrapped around a metal pipe. At room temperature, the resistance is so high that the light bulb in the hood hardly glows at all.

cury, although the temperature at which the transition to zero resistance occurs for each metal is different. But the essential point—that in some materials it is possible to do away with electrical resistance entirely—is firmly established.

In a superconductor, there is no way for an electrical current to lose energy. Whatever current exists in a superconductor must continue to flow unabated, whether there is a power source connected to the superconductor or not. For example, if we connect a battery to a coil of superconducting material, let a current build up in the material, and then disconnect the battery, the current will continue to flow. Since there is no way for the electrons that constitute the current to lose their energy, the current in the coil will keep going, quite literally, forever. In fact, there is a loop of superconductor in Leiden in which just such a current has been flowing for more than fifty years, without any measurable diminution.

When the copper wire is immersed in liquid nitrogen, its resistance drops and the bulb glows brighter and brighter. Photos by Judith Peatross.

The fact that a superconductor can support these persistent currents suggests the most important and likeliest application of this strange effect. In chapter 6 we learned that an electrical current flowing in a loop gives rise to a magnetic field indistinguishable from that associated with an ordinary permanent magnet. For a loop made of ordinary wire, we have to pump in current continuously with a battery or generator to make up for the energy loss due to resistance. Hence, an ordinary electromagnet, whether a large industrial model or the ignition coil in your car, must be connected continuously to a power source whenever you want to utilize its magnetic field. An important limitation on the size of the magnetic field we can produce with an ordinary electromagnet comes from the fact that heat generated in this way has to be continually removed. Otherwise it will melt the magnet. Thus, it is necessary to pump large amounts of cooling water through pipes in the body of the magnet, an operation analogous to the cooling system of your car.

With a superconducting magnet, however, no power is needed to overcome resistance, so that once the initial current is set in motion, the magnet operates without being plugged in. The only maintenance cost is keeping the magnet at a temperature a few degrees above absolute zero, a task that is easily carried out by using modern techniques similar to the thermos bottle. For the first time, we have available a relatively inexpensive source of very strong magnetic fields.

Until very recently, the major use of superconducting magnets was in the construction of particle accelerators, such as that at the Fermi National Accelerator Laboratory near Chicago. These machines are used to boost protons to speeds only a fraction less than the speed of light and then smash them into stationary targets. Most of the knowledge we have gained about the ultimate structure of matter has come through the use of such machines. In order to impart this kind of energy to the protons, a structure like that in Illustration 74 is used. A large ring is built and surrounded by magnets. When protons are inserted into a ring of this sort, the

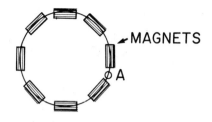

Illustration 74

magnets exert forces that keep the protons moving in a circle and thus keep them in the ring. If there were nothing in the accelerator but the magnets, the protons would continue to circulate at a constant speed, and the only energy used would be that required to keep the magnets "live." Under normal circumstances, however, every time the protons come to a particular spot on the ring (such as that labeled *A* in the illustration), an electronic device gives them a small boost in energy. Over many cycles, these small boosts add up to very high energies indeed.

But the really amazing thing about an accelerator like this is its size. The Fermilab machine, for example, is almost a mile across, which means that it has to be lined with about three miles of magnets. In the first phase of construction of the machine conventional electromagnets were used, and when the machine was running at full capacity, just keeping these magnets going consumed a noticeable fraction of the power available in the Illinois grid. In many laboratories, the cost of power has led to periods when a machine is simply turned off for lack of money to pay the electric bill.

A program is now under way at Fermilab to install a second ring of magnets (essentially doubling the energy that can be imparted to the protons). This time around, however, the magnets will be superconducting, making this the largest installation of superconductors in the world. In 1983, when the "energy doubler" is scheduled to be turned on, a major milestone in the transition of superconductivity from a laboratory curiosity to a practical every-

The tunnel of the main accelerator at Fermilab, in Batavia, Illinois. The upper ring of magnets is the 400 BeV accelerator. The lower ring shows the magnets for the superconducting accelerator being installed. Photo courtesy of the Fermi National Accelerator Laboratory.

day tool will have been passed. As often happens with high-technology items, most of this development was funded as part of the federal basic research effort.

Projects like the Fermilab energy doubler show that it is perfectly feasible to introduce large-scale factory-style manufacturing to the production of superconducting magnets. There are already several small firms producing them in the United States. A typical commercial superconducting magnet is made from an alloy of niobium and tin and immersed in liquid helium at about 4 degrees above absolute zero during operation.

The French TGV or trains à grande vitesse, *which travel at 200 miles per hour.* Photo courtesy of the French National Railroads.

But while the research uses of superconducting magnets are the single largest market for this technology today, the most exciting future prospects are in the field of mass transportation. Right now the limit on the speed of a passenger train is between one hundred and two hundred miles per hour and is set by the friction between the wheels of the train and the tracks. The French TGV *(trains à grande vitesse)* travel at 200 miles per hour, and most engineers agree that this represents about the best that can be done with conventional trains.

The availability of superconducting magnets, however, introduces an interesting new possibility. If we could use the magnetic force to lift the train off the ground, then wheels would not be needed and the top speed of the train could be increased considerably. A sketch of how such a train might be designed is shown in Illustration 75. The train rides on a metal guide. Inside the

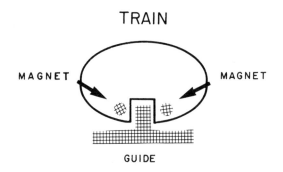

TRAIN

MAGNET   MAGNET

GUIDE

Illustration 75

train body is a set of superconducting magnets. When at rest the train rides on rubber wheels. As the train starts moving, however, a force develops between the magnets and the guide bar, which is somewhat similar to that between two magnets, and the train "lifts off"—quite literally levitates several inches off the track. With no wheel friction, the train can now be accelerated to speeds comparable to those achieved by aircraft.

Although the United States and Germany are both working on this idea, the world leader in the development of "maglev" (for "magnetic levitation") is Japan. At their test track near Miyazaki in southern Japan, Japanese railroads have run full-size prototypes at speeds above 325 miles per hour! Trains of this type could move passengers from downtown Washington, D.C., to New York City in less than an hour—about the time required for an airliner to fly from one airport to the other. And, because superconductors are basically very energy efficient, they could do so at a fraction of the cost in energy now required.

Visionaries such as Robert Salter at the Rand Corporation are thinking beyond this sort of train to a truly revolutionary transportation system based on superconductivity. Just as the wheel friction sets the upper speed limit on a conventional train, the drag of the air through which the train moves sets the limit on how fast a maglev train can go. Salter envisions the next step in ground travel to be a maglev train running in a tunnel from which the air has been exhausted. He calculates that such trains could achieve speeds of six thousand miles per hour, making the trip across the continental United States in less than an hour. Whether a monumental engineering job such as a cross-country tunnel will ever be undertaken is an open question, of course, but the fact that you can talk about it at all indicates the tremendous potential of the new superconducting technology.

But this excursion into the world of future technology does little to enlighten us about the very basic question we posed when we first discussed the phenomenon of superconductivity—how a superconductor can exist at all. It wasn't until 1957, a half century after Onnes' discovery, that three American physicists succeeded in providing an explanation. For this achievement John Bardeen, Leon Cooper, and J. Robert Schrieffer were awarded the Nobel Prize in physics in 1972.

Think of a single electron moving through a lattice of heavy ions as shown in Illustration 76. When it passes between a pair of

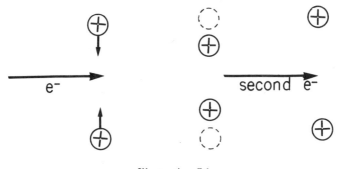

Illustration 76

ions, the electrical forces will tend to pull the ions toward it, as shown. The electron is not affected because the forces exerted by the ions cancel each other, but the electron moves so swiftly that it is long gone by the time the ponderous ions can respond to it. This response takes the form shown in the middle diagram: After the passage of the first electron, we have two positively charged ions closer together in its wake than they would ordinarily be. Given enough time, the ions would return to their original positions, of course, but momentarily there is a concentration of positive charge at that point in the metal, and this tends to attract electrons.

A second electron, attracted to the concentration of positive charge, will thus follow along after the first. The two form what is known as a Cooper pair and proceed in tandem through the solid. In a typical material, there will be several hundred heavy ions between the front and back member of the pair, so that the electrical repulsion between the two has little effect on their behavior.

When the temperature of the metal falls below the point where this delicate mechanism isn't completely masked by the thermal motion of the ions, the electrons tend to form pairs as they move through the conductor. Furthermore, all the free electrons form pairs of this sort, so that the conductor becomes saturated with overlapping electron pairs.

Because of the large distances between the members of a Cooper pair, the pairs within a given material will overlap each other, as in Illustration 77. If you think of each strand of spaghetti

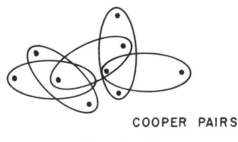

COOPER PAIRS

Illustration 77

in a bowl as a Cooper pair with an electron on each end, the relation between the pairs is pretty well represented by the tangled interlocking of the spaghetti. If a single electron in such a web encounters an ion in the solid, the only way the ion can deflect the electron is to deflect the entire web.

An analogy should make this point clear. A single car moving down a highway will bounce and perhaps even be deflected when it encounters a pothole. If we had a fleet of cars moving down the highway, however, and if the members of that fleet were all welded together, such a deflection would not occur. The fleet would simply ride roughshod over the pothole, and the single cars that encountered it would be carried across it by the joint motion of the fleet.

In the same way, a single electron encountering an ion can lose energy and generate heat, but those locked in a collection of Cooper pairs will go right by without any change. The phenomenon of superconductivity can thus be explained by reference to the formation of pairs between the free electrons in the conductor.

The most important lesson we can learn from the light bulb may be this: simple descriptions of the behavior of systems in one domain (for example, the region of normal temperatures) may need to be replaced by completely different and unexpected processes in another. Since we can never tell when a new phenomenon might be of great practical use, it always pays to push the frontiers of knowledge as far as they can be pushed, even though there seems to be little probability of a practical payoff when we start exploring. After all, if someone had told Kammerlingh Onnes that his experiments on resistance at low temperatures might someday lead to vast improvements in mass transit, he would doubtless have been highly skeptical.

10

What Would
a Giant Look Like?

MANY YEARS AGO AN ADVENTURE SERIES CALLED "LAND OF THE Giants" was seen regularly by TV viewers. The plot was simple: a spaceship full of human beings crash lands on a planet inhabited by beings that look just like us, but are thirty to forty feet tall. The show centered on the crew's adventures as they lived in the walls of the giants' homes.

It was, of course, easy to raise obvious objections to the program. It was pointed out that there was a very low probability that a race of giant extraterrestrials would be found living in something that looked suspiciously like a suburb of Los Angeles. At a deeper level, the essential assumption of the script—that giants' bodies would have pretty much the same shape and proportions as ours—touches on a very old difficulty in science, the problem of scale.

Practical people have known for a long time that building

something bigger cannot be done just by making every part bigger in proportion. For example, it is not possible to make a good cargo ship by taking a successful rowboat design and making every part ten times larger. As the absolute size of anything increases, there have to be substantial changes in the basic design. Nature exhibits this as well. An elephant is larger than an ant, but it is also markedly different in its proportions. The same statement could be made about a stone house and a cathedral. The question of why there should be such a change in proportion as the size of a three-dimensional structure is increased is known as the problem of scale, and we'll have to understand the principles involved if we want to think about giants.

Galileo first saw how to solve the problem. He was a man of great practical achievements and spent much of his time working on engineering and military problems. One of these was the disturbing tendency of large machines to break down when they were copied from designs for very successful smaller models. In 1638, four years before his death, Galileo published a book titled *Dialogues Concerning the Two New Sciences*. The second part of the book dealt with the motions of projectiles and is widely regarded as a major advance in the development of physics. The first part, "New Science," is usually passed over by modern commentators. Yet in this dialogue Galileo solved the problem of scale and thereby cleared the way for important advances in engineering.

He sets the stage by having Sagretio, one of the participants in the dialogue, comment, "If a large machine be constructed in such a way that its parts bear to one another the same ratio as in a smaller one, and if the smaller is sufficiently strong for the purpose for which it was designed, I do not see why the larger should not be able to withstand any severe test to which it may be subjected." Sagretio then launches into a discussion of the fact that workers at that great shipyard called the Arsenal of Venice had noticed that scaffolding for large ships had to be built from much larger logs than a simple scaling up of the small scaffolding would suggest.

Rather than follow Galileo's discussion, we can come to the

heart of the matter by thinking about a cube of material one foot on a side. Depending on the material, the weight of such a cube could be 64 pounds (water), 482 pounds (steel), or 10^{15} pounds (a cube made up entirely of atomic nuclei). The pressure on the bottom face of the cube will be the weight of the cube divided by the area of the bottom face. For steel, the bottom face of the cube will be subjected to a pressure of 492 pounds per square foot. This is a relatively mild pressure for a steel structure, somewhat less than that of the air in a normal automobile tire. There would be no possibility that the cube would collapse under its own weight.

But suppose we double all the dimensions of the cube. The new cube (see Illustration 78) will measure two feet on a side. The volume of the cube will now be $2 \times 2 \times 2 = 8$ times the volume of the original cube, and thus its weight will be 3,936 pounds. On the other hand, the cross-sectional area of the bottom face of the new cube will be $2 \times 2 = 4$ square feet, so that the pressure on the bottom face of the doubled cube will now be 984 pounds per square foot—twice what it was in the original. This numerical exercise, simple as it is, contains the solution of the problem of scale.

Starting with the 2-foot cube, let us continue the operation of doubling the sides. The next step (shown on the right in Illustration 78) would be a cube measuring 4 feet on a side. It would weigh 31,488 pounds and have a pressure of 1,968 pounds per

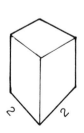
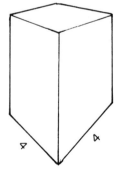

Illustration 78

square foot at the base. It's easy to see that each time we double the dimensions of the cube, we also double the pressure exerted on each square foot of the bottom face. Eventually, this process reaches a limit. With steel, when we have a cube slightly over four miles on a side, the force of gravity acting on the steel will produce a force on the bottom face sufficient to overcome the forces that hold the atoms in the material together, and the steel along the bottom of the cube will crumble. In technical language, we say that the pressure due to the weight of the steel in the cube exceeds the tensile strength of steel so that the metal fractures. From this example, we see that the argument put forward by Sagretio must be wrong. We know that a 1-foot cube is perfectly capable of sustaining its own weight, but we can calculate that a scaled-up cube four miles on a side will not be a stable structure. The larger cube fails the simplest possible mechanical test—supporting its own weight. There is no hope that it would be able to pass a "severe test" as Sagretio expected.

From this example, the solution to the problem of scale is obvious. The key point is that the volume of material (and hence its weight) increases faster than the cross-sectional area that must support that weight. In the case of our cube, the volume goes up by a factor of 8 whenever the length of a side is doubled, but the area of the base goes up by only a factor of 4. One simple way to visualize this effect is to imagine doubling the dimensions of the cube by adding blocks to the original (see Illustration 79). In order

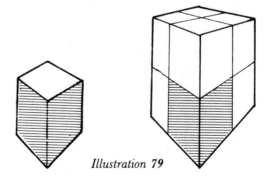

Illustration 79

to produce a doubled cube in this way, we have to add seven more cubes, each 1 foot on a side. This makes a total of eight cubes, four on the front face and four on the back.

As far as the original cube is concerned, all that the doubling process does is pile an additional cube on top of it. This, in turn, means that the original cube must now support not only its own weight, but that of the new cube as well. Doubling the scale of the structure therefore doubles the weight resting on the original cube while doing nothing to increase its ability to support that weight. Each doubling compounds this situation until the fracture point is reached.

Going from a 1-foot steel cube to something four miles on a side involves scaling up by a factor of about 20,000, a pretty big increase in anybody's book. Scaling up from an ant to an elephant involves a factor of several thousand, a roughly comparable enlargement.

As to the giants with which we began, scaling up a 6-foot human being to 30 feet would involve an increase in pressure on the bones of a factor of 5. Human bones have a safety factor of about 150—that is, the fracture limit of the bone is about 150 times the weight that the bone is normally expected to carry. Because broken bones are not uncommon, we can conclude that this ratio is a compromise between strength and the ability of the organism to move easily. In a scaled-up giant, this safety factor would go down to 30.

If our giants are not to spend a large part of their time recovering from broken bones, a simple scaling up of the dimensions of an ordinary human being just won't do. The problem is to find a way of increasing body mass without exceeding the strength limits of the structural material, in this case bone matter. There are a number of ways that the problem can be solved. In architecture, different materials, with greater strength, are used in large buildings. A wooden building will rarely exceed 50 feet in height, nor will a stone building go beyond a few hundred. The massive boom in skyscraper construction that has marked urban architecture in our century was made possible by the development of mass-produced steel for I-beams. Using modern steels, buildings of well over 1,000 feet can be built. In each case, the amount of material that can be piled up over a given square foot of floor space before strength limits are reached is increased by changing the material that has to do the supporting. Nature itself has often followed this rule. The ant-to-elephant scaling we referred to operates at least in part by the substitution of the elephant's interior skeleton made of calcium for the more fragile exterior casing of the ant.

But another strategy can be used that does not involve the use of new materials. Suppose we think about doubling the cube in a slightly different way. What if we ask, "How can we put together a structure made of eight cubes of steel and not double the load on the bottom surface?" One answer is shown in Illustration 80. If

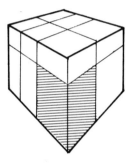

Illustration 80

we cut two of the cubes in thirds, we can put together a pile of steel with six cubes along the bottom and 1⅓ cubes high. The weight of steel above each square foot in this arrangement is only 656 pounds, significantly less than the 984 pounds in the doubled cube.

Of course, the new arrangement is no longer a cube; the sides are rectangular instead of square. It incorporates the same amount of material as a doubled cube, but there is much less pressure on the lower face. This suggests that one way of making bigger structures is to change the proportions as the size grows. The more material to be included, the squatter and broader the structure will have to be.

That nature has also taken this route is obvious from the comparison of the proportion of a human being and an elephant. Since the tensile strength of the material of the bones in human beings and in elephants is roughly the same, a change in proportions is the way to achieve a significant increase in size.

A 30-foot giant would be five times as large in every dimension as a 6-foot human being. It would therefore weigh 125 times as much, so that a 200-pound man made five times larger would weigh over 12 tons, Since this is more than the weight of an elephant, there is no possibility that anything this massive could have anything like the dimensions of a human being.

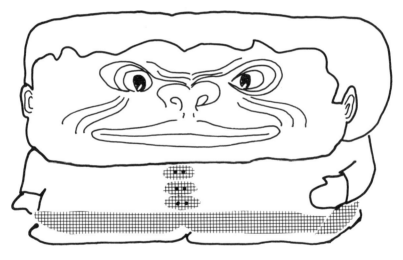

Illustration 81

For the sake of argument, assume that we want to design a 12-ton giant whose skeleton is to be made from material like human bone, and suppose that we want to keep the safety factor of the skeleton above 100. The giant would have to be 9 feet tall, 8 feet from front to back, and 16 feet wide! He would look more like a Sherman tank than a person, and probably wouldn't make a very good character in a TV series.

Once we understand the way scaling works, all sorts of amusing things can be done. For example, numbered among my faults is an addiction to old science-fiction movies. One of my favorites, *The Beginning of the End,* concerns a race of giant grasshoppers spawned in Illinois by experiments with radioactivity. For lack of anything better to do, the grasshoppers attack Chicago, whose inhabitants are saved only by the last-minute exploits of the hero and his beautiful assistant. Since a normal grasshopper is approximately 2 inches long, producing one 50 feet long would involve a scaling factor of 300. Assuming that the grasshopper's exoskeleton has the same safety factor as human bones (150), a 50-foot grasshopper, far from constituting a threat to the city of Chicago and the heroine, would simply collapse under its own weight. Too bad—it made a terrific movie.

On another level, we can extend the idea of the largest possible cube of steel to something more familiar. We can ask how tall a mountain on the surface of the earth could be before it collapsed. The density of granite is only about 40 percent that of steel, and the tensile strength is half as much. Using the same reasoning as before, but substituting granite for steel, would lead to a maximum size for a mountain of 7 miles. This is not far from the actual 6-mile height of the largest mountains on earth.

In all these suppositions, we are dealing with the field of study called strength of materials. We have seen how to calculate the effects of scaling, but we have not yet attempted to deal with the problem at a more fundamental level. It should be possible to discuss topics like the maximum size of a mountain in terms of the properties of the atoms that compose materials, rather than in terms of empirically measured quantities like tensile strength. In addition, there are a number of regularities in the properties of materials that can only be explained by reference to atomic structure. For example, we know that the densities of most solids range between one and ten times that of water. Why should this be so? We also know that the pressure required to deform most solids is between 100,000 and one miliion times the pressure normally exerted by the atmosphere. Why? To answer questions like these, we must examine the atom itself.

We know that the nucleus of an atom is very small compared to the size of the electron orbits. Indeed, if the nucleus of a typical atom were the size of a bowling ball, then its electrons could be thought of as a handful of peas scattered over an area the size of a large city. Consequently, we expect that the interactions of an atom with its neighbors will be dominated by the electrons, since they will be the first part of the atom to be encountered.

In chapter 4 we learned that many properties of the electron can be described if we think of it as a wave rather than a particle. We can, accordingly, learn something about the way an electron behaves when confined within an atom by thinking about other kinds of confined waves that are easier to visualize. Perhaps the most familiar example of a confined wave is water sloshing around in a bathtub. There the wave is moving, but it is reflected by the solid walls of the tub. Another familiar example is the vibration of a plucked string—on a guitar, for example. We speak of the up-and-down vibration of the string as a standing wave, as opposed to a traveling wave. Both kinds of waves obviously possess energy, since in the bathtub the particles of water are moving, and in the guitar the particles in the string are doing the same. The kinetic energy of these particles is what we mean when we talk about the energy of the wave. We have also learned that anything possessing energy is capable of doing work (i.e., of exerting a force through a distance), and this is as true of waves as of anything else.

An electron confined to an atom is best thought of as a standing wave, and, hence, is more like the guitar string than the bathtub wave. At the same time, we know that an electron will sooner or later wind up in an orbit where its total energy is at a minimum. The two competing effects that we know must exist to produce this minimum are easy to understand. Think of an electron in an orbit of a given radius. There are two components to its energy: the electrical potential energy that arises because the electron and nucleus are of opposite charge, and the energy associated with the electron wave. If we moved the electron to an orbit with a smaller radius, the electrical potential energy would decrease but the kinetic energy of the wave would increase. The latter statement corresponds to saying that shrinking the size of the bathtub would cause the water in it to move around more violently, and this in turn would increase the energy of the wave. The electron will settle in an orbit where these two effects balance and the energy is minimized.

It turns out that for a single electron going around a single proton (the hydrogen atom), this radius is found at about .75 $\times$ 10^{-8} cm. We would expect, then, that this should be roughly the size of an atom. Atoms with more electrons will be larger, of course, but even uranium with its ninety-two electrons has a radius of about 2.2 $\times$ 10^{-8} cm—only about three times as large. To a first approximation, then, all atoms are roughly the same size.

Thinking in this way about the structure of an atom leads to the conclusion that atoms must be roughly 10^{-8} cm in radius. This can shed some light on the fact that the densities of all solids seem to be comparable. In a solid, atoms are packed together like marbles filling a box. There is very little "wasted" space between them. If we think of each atom as a sphere whose radius we call R_A, then the volume of a single atom will be $\frac{4\pi}{3}R_A^3$. The mass of an atom, on the other hand, resides almost entirely in the nucleus. Since each proton and neutron has a mass of about 1.7 $\times$ 10^{-24} grams each, the mass of the atom will be this number multiplied by the total number of protons and neutrons in the nucleus (a number customarily denoted by the letter A; A is 1 for hydrogen and 238 for uranium).

Every solid is made up of a large but finite number of atoms. Call this number N. The total mass of the solid will then be N times the mass of one atom, while the total volume will be roughly N times the volume of that atom. The density of the solid, by definition, will be its total mass divided by its total volume.

If we take hydrogen as an example, $A = 1$ and R_A is $.75 \times 10^{-8}$ cm. The density of solid hydrogen should be

$$\rho_H = \frac{N \times 1.7 \times 10^{-24} \text{ gm}}{N \times 1.7 \times 10^{-25} \text{ cm}^3} \approx 1 \text{ gm/cc}$$

which is approximately the density of water. Uranium, on the other hand, has $A = 238$ and $R_A = 2.2 \times 10^{-8}$ cm. Its density will be

$$\rho_u = \frac{N \times 238 \times 1.7 \times 10^{-24} \text{ gm}}{N \times 4.5 \times 10^{-23}} = 9.0 \text{ gm/cm}^3$$

This is slightly less than ten times the density of water.

From this exercise, we see that the reason the densities of solids are so alike is related to the fact that the overall size of an atom must be of the order of 10^{-8} cm, while the mass of the atom is some multiple of the mass of the proton. Dividing this sort of mass by this sort of volume will always give a number in the neighborhood of 1–10 grams/cc. That there are no metals much denser than lead and uranium and no solids much less dense than water is related to the fundamental quantities of atomic physics in a simple way.

Before going on, there is one possible point of confusion about this argument that should be explained. We have calculated the density of solids by assuming that the atoms are closely packed together and that there is no open space between them. This does not, however, mean we have assumed that atoms are themselves solid. We know that atoms are largely empty space. Nevertheless, solids are constructed in such a way that there is little or no overlap between neighboring atoms, and this is the basis of our calculation.

Ultimately, the strength of any material is related to how well it can withstand external forces. To a certain extent, this will depend on the way the material is put together. We have seen in chapter 9 how one class of solids—conducting metals—is arranged. In such metals there is a lattice of positive ions, each of which has contributed one electron to a negatively charged sea. Each electron moves through the lattice independently of the atom that originally donated it.

From our previous discussion, we know that the electrons in metals will move around; they will therefore have kinetic energy and be capable of exerting a pressure by means of collisions (see chapter 7 for a detailed discussion of how pressure can be generated in this way). If we think of the electrons as waves, however, our first impression is that they have plenty of room to move. Each electron would be a wave confined in the entire piece of material, a situation somewhat analogous to turning a bathtub wave loose in the ocean. If this were true, we might expect the pressure exerted by the electrons to be quite small.

Yet one fact about electrons that we haven't encountered negates this conclusion. It turns out that electrons have to obey a rule called the Pauli principle, which states that no two electrons can be in the same state. (The term *state* has a rather specialized meaning when applied to particles like the electron. For our purposes, we will assume that we have defined the state of an electron in a solid when we have specified its velocity and sense of spin.) The principle is named after its discoverer, Austrian physicist Wolfgang Pauli, who received the Nobel Prize in 1945. In the case of a metal, this means that if one electron at one point in the metal is moving with a certain speed in a certain direction, rotating about its axis in a particular way, then nowhere else in the metal can there be another electron with just that velocity and rotation. Since there are over 10^{26} electrons in a piece of metal the size of a thimble, those states of the electron that correspond to a wave rattling around in the entire metal will be filled quickly, and other electrons will have to have wavelengths corresponding to much shorter distances.

One way to think of the Pauli principle is to compare the electrons to cars in a parking lot. Once a car has filled a slot, no other car can occupy it. In this way, the parking lot is "full" in the sense that long before every square inch in the lot is occupied no more cars can be accommodated. Electrons in a metal follow the same rule; they, too, fill up available states long before you might expect them to.

The practical effect of the Pauli principle for the strength of a metal is that each electron has, on the average, an energy appropriate to a wave confined to a much smaller volume. Even though each electron is free to wander through the positive lattice, the presence of other electrons squeezes it in and confines its wave to a volume roughly comparable to the volume of a single atom. Since we saw that the energy of a confined wave increases as its dimensions are reduced, the Pauli principle has the effect of greatly increasing the pressure due to the free electrons in a metal.

If we put in numbers for a typical metal, we find that the electron pressure is huge, something like 100,000 times that of the atmosphere. This pressure inside the metal would blow it apart instantly if it weren't canceled by something else. The force that opposes the pressure is the electrical attraction between the electrons and the ions. The best way to visualize this is to think of the electrons in the metal as a gas under high pressure, with the positive ions as a stationary lattice fixed in space. If the electron gas started to expand under its own pressure the way an ordinary gas would, the electrical force exerted by the positive ions would quickly pull it back in. Even though each electron is free to roam through the metal, the electrons as a whole are chained to the material by intense electrical forces. Our picture of a metal, then, is one in which two very large forces act in opposing directions to create an equilibrium. The electrical force tends to pull the electrons in and make the metal contract while the electron pressure tends to blow it apart.

If we try to compress a metal with an external force, we are, in effect, trying to shrink the volume in which the electron waves find themselves. To do this, we must overcome the pressure that these waves exert. This, in turn, means that we would expect that solids would hold their shape until pressures comparable to

100,000 atmospheres are attained. This is what is observed in nature. The so-called bulk modulus (the quantity that measures the response of a material to pressure) is about the same for most solids and corresponds to external pressures between 100,000 and one million atmospheres, as our reasoning suggested it should.

The tensile strength of materials, a quantity central to our discussion of the problem of scale, is more difficult to estimate from first principles. The way a piece of material will react when it experiences a force in one direction, but is free to move in other directions, depends on many things (such as the existence of microscopic faults and other defects), which are hard to calculate. In general, the pressure needed to crumble the bottom face of a block of steel is 1 to 10 percent of the pressure needed to force the steel to change its shape uniformly.

The pressure exerted by electrons when they are free to move is called degeneracy pressure. We have seen that we should think of the electrons as a sort of gas pervading the material, and the pressure that they exert as analogous to that exerted by the air inside an inflated tire. But earthly solids are not the only place where such pressures are important in nature. There are many objects of interest to astronomers where it plays a role. Consider the sun as a typical star. It maintains the shape it has because of the competition of two effects. One is the gravitational attraction between its various parts, an effect which, if unchecked, would cause it to collapse upon itself. The countervailing force is generated in the nuclear reactions in the core of the sun. As the energy from this reaction percolates outward it exerts a pressure that cancels the inward pull of gravity, preventing a collapse. For another five billion years or so, this same thing will be going on and the sun will maintain pretty nearly its present size. Eventually, however, it will run out of nuclear fuel and, after a series of transitional stages, it will start to shrink as the force of gravity reasserts itself. It will continue to collapse until something else arises to provide the countervailing force.

As you may have guessed by now, that something is the

degeneracy pressure of the sun's electrons. Without its source of nuclear fuel, the sun will collapse until the inward force of gravity cannot compress the electron gas any further. We can estimate what the radius of the sun will be when this happens in much the same way that we estimated the size of the atom. The sun has a mass of 2×10^{30} Kg, so that using the mass of the proton given above, we see that it must have roughly 10^{57} protons. Since the sun is electrically neutral, it must have about this number of electrons as well. In the sun the temperatures are so high that all of these electrons have been stripped from their atoms and constitute just the kind of electron gas we've been attributing to metals. To calculate the size of the future sun, we simply ask to what radius an electron gas of this size must be compressed before the pressure it exerts will counteract the force of gravity (which, the sun being then much smaller and denser, will be significantly higher than it is at the solar surface today). When this calculation is made, we find that the resulting star will be a few tens of thousands of miles across—about the size of the earth. It will be of the kind called a white dwarf, and its condition will exemplify the fate of most stars the size of the sun.

If a star were much more massive than the sun to begin with, the electron pressure would never be enough to stop the collapse. The star's radius would quickly move down past the thousand-mile mark, to the point where gravitational pressures are so great that the electrons are literally forced into the protons, forming a small but incredibly massive body of solid neutron matter. Neutrons, like electrons, obey the Pauli principle, but they are almost two thousand times as heavy. This difference between the two particles means that a neutron gas would have to be compressed to a volume several thousand times smaller than the corresponding electron gas in order to exert the same pressure. For large stars, then, the failure of the electron pressure to balance gravity means that the collapse will proceed until a body a few tens of miles across is formed. At this point, the star is composed almost entirely of neutrons. Appropriately enough, it is called a neutron star. Many such objects have been observed in the heavens.

If the star is massive enough for gravity to overcome the neutron pressure the way electron pressure was overcome on the way to the neutron star, there is nothing left to stop it, and the star continues to collapse until it becomes an object called a black hole. Once a black hole is formed, gravitational forces near it are so strong that nothing—not even light—can ever get out again.

Our talk of giants has led us to white dwarfs, neutron stars, and black holes—some of the most exotic objects in the universe.

11

Why Is the Sky Blue?

I SAW A STUDY RECENTLY IN WHICH A DEVELOPMENTAL PSYCHOL-
ogist claimed that children around three years of age ask more
than four hundred questions in a single day. No one who has been
a parent would be inclined to dispute this figure—indeed, some
might say it was too low. The "blue sky" question is typical of the
sort of thing a child might ask. It involves a familiar phenomenon,
something we see every day, and yet the answer demands some
fairly sophisticated thinking.

The problem is compounded by another fact that has become
common knowledge in the past decade. Above the earth's atmosphere, the sky isn't blue, but pitch black. Films taken from earth-
orbiting satellites and the space shuttle have made this part of
every youngster's arsenal of facts, and it's something that we have
to explain.

The difference in the appearance of the sky when viewed

from above and below the earth's atmosphere suggests that the answer to our question is going to lead us into an investigation of the way that light interacts with matter (and more particularly the matter that constitutes the earth's atmosphere). We already know from the discussion of interference in chapter 4 that it is useful to describe light as a wave in most familiar situations. The matter with which sunlight interacts in the atmosphere can be divided into two categories. First, there are molecules of oxygen, nitrogen, and other gases. These molecules are typically many thousand times smaller than the wavelength of light. At the same time, there are many kinds of particles floating in the air, as we have learned to our sorrow in this environmentally conscious age. These particles are much larger than the wavelength of light. To explain the color of the sky, then, we have to think about the behavior of a light wave that encounters a medium composed of a mixture of very large and very small objects, where *large* and *small* are defined relative to the wavelength of light.

The best way to approach this problem is to imagine an analogous situation with a wave you can visualize. Suppose you are standing on a cliff overlooking the ocean, watching the surf coming toward the beach. On a typical day, the distance between crests (i.e., the wavelength) might be ten feet. If there is a rock just offshore, we would have a situation like the one shown in Illustration 82. The incoming surf would move past the rock, but a second wave centered on the rock would be produced as well. We say that the rock scatters the incoming wave, and the wave that moves out in concentric circles from the rock is called the scattered wave. We shall see that a similar scattering is the crucial process in the explanation of the blue sky.

In this analogy, the incoming surf plays the role of the sunlight falling on the earth's atmosphere, and the rock plays the role of the matter it encounters there. But the analogy is not exact, as our discussion of the contents of the atmosphere has shown. An offshore rock of the type shown in Illustration 82 might be anywhere from a few feet to tens of feet across—roughly the same dimension as the wavelength of the surf being scattered. In the

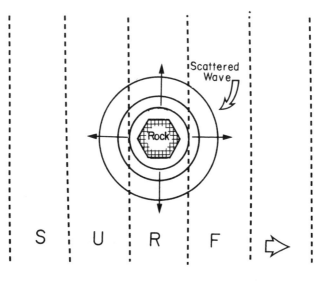

Illustration 82

atmosphere, however, the scattering centers are proportionately much smaller or much larger than the wavelengths of the light.

We know that a molecule in the air is about a thousand times smaller than the wavelength of visible light. In our example, in which there is surf with a ten-foot wavelength, a scattering center analagous to an air molecule would be a "rock" one-eighth of an inch across—about twice the size of the lead in a pencil. Thus, molecules in the air would be analogous to a forest of thin needles in the surf.

The particulate matter in the air, by contrast, comes in clumps anywhere from fifty to many thousands of times the wavelength of light. The analog of such a particle would be a "rock" slightly bigger than a city block.

Therefore, asking about the way the sky appears to a person on the ground is equivalent to asking about the patterns of the waves that reach the beach after coming through an "atmosphere" made up of thickly distributed needles interspersed with occasional huge rocks.

It will be easiest for us to consider these two components of the atmosphere separately. This is particularly appropriate because, as we shall see shortly, the details of the way light is scattered from these two types of obstructions differ significantly.

Light is an electromagnetic wave, which means that the wave consists of an oscillating electrical field in much the same way that a water wave consists of an oscillating liquid surface. The atoms in the molecule on which this wave impinges can be thought of as a light, negatively charged electron attached by a spring to a very heavy positive nucleus. When the oscillating electrical field hits the atom, the electron jiggles up and down, just as a cork might bob up and down in the surf. But in this collision the nucleus of the atom moves very little because of its mass (think of it as anchored). The effect of the light on the atom, then, is to force only the electron to move up and down rapidly.

An electron accelerated in this way will emit radiation. The greater the acceleration, the greater will be the intensity of the radiation. In a similar way, the electrons pushed back and forth through an antenna wire produce radio and TV transmissions. If the electron is jiggled at the proper frequencies, it will emit light instead of radio waves. This scattered light will move out from the atom in concentric circles, exactly analogously to the water wave scattering out from the rock.

We can get closer to the blue sky answer by thinking a little more about the way the electron is tied to the atom. If you have a reasonably stiff spring and you want to jiggle a weight at the end of it back and forth, you know that there will be one frequency at which it will be very easy to do. If you try to jiggle it slower or faster than this so-called resonant frequency, you have to do more work to make the spring move the way you want it to, and the farther away from the resonant frequency you are, the more energy it takes to move the end of the spring.

In the atmosphere, incoming light is trying to move the end of the spring. In this case the resonant frequency—the frequency at which it is easiest to move the electron around—occurs in the ultraviolet region, well out of the visible range. This means that light at frequencies near the blue end of the spectrum will have an easier time moving electrons in atoms than will light at the lower frequencies near the red end, simply because blue light is closer to the resonant frequency.

We expect, then, that an electron in an atom on which blue light impinges will be accelerated more than an electron in an identical atom bathed in red light. Since the intensity of the light emitted by the electron depends on the acceleration, and since it is the emitted light we identify as the scattered wave, we expect that atmospheric molecules will have an easier time producing scattered waves from blue light than from red. Thus, a beam of blue light directed into the atmosphere will travel a relatively short distance before it is completely scattered by the atomic electrons, while a beam of red light will travel much farther before it meets a similar fate.

In terms of our analogy with the surf, the needles in the water have the property of producing scattered waves much more readily from surf that has a short wavelength (i.e., waves where the crests are close together) than from surf with a long wavelength. If we imagine our forest of needles stretching many miles out to sea, it follows that much more of the original surf will get to the beach on days when there are long intervals between the crests than on days when there are not.

We now note one more important fact. Viewed above the atmosphere, the sun appears to be white; it produces light at roughly equal intensities across the entire visible spectrum from red to blue. If you think of the light coming from the sun as a mixture of beams of all the different colors, then the argument we just went through means that the beams corresponding to colors near the blue end of the spectrum will be scattered out of the direct sunlight relatively soon, and that the beams corresponding to colors near the red end will tend to remain whole. With this knowledge, we can not only answer the blue sky question, but explain some other common observations as well.

All the light that enters the earth's atmosphere comes from the sun. That we can see light when we look in directions away from the sun implies we are seeing light that has been scattered out of the direct sunlight. This, in turn, means that light coming from any direction other than the sun will tend to be blue, since air molecules scatter blue light most readily.

This also explains why the sky as seen from the space shuttle in orbit or from the surface of the moon is not blue, but black. If there is no atmosphere to scatter sunlight, then there will be nothing like the scattered wave shown in Illustration 83. Someone

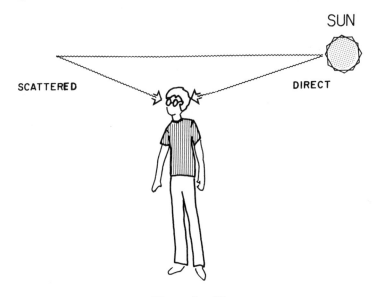

Illustration 83

looking away from the sun will see no light at all and will report a black sky with a few stars in it. That light can reach us only by being scattered (unless we look directly at the source) is familiar to those who have been in an airplane landing after dark in rainy weather. When the plane's landing lights are turned on, we don't normally see them from the cabin windows because the beam is directed straight ahead. When the plane moves through some falling rain, however, light is scattered by the drops and the beam suddenly becomes visible. The effect is to make the beam alternately visible and invisible to the passenger.

Returning to the question of the appearance of the sky, we know that the light that comes directly through the atmosphere without being scattered will be the original white sunlight with the colors at the blue end of the spectrum taken out of the beam. Hence, the farther the sunlight has to travel through the atmosphere to reach our eyes, the more it will appear to be shifted away from the blue end. When the sun is overhead, there is relatively little atmosphere to be traversed, so the daytime sun has a yellow color. At sunset, however, we are looking at the sun through a much longer path in the air; more of the higher-frequency light will be scattered out of the beam, and the sun will appear to be red. This situation is shown in Illustration 84.

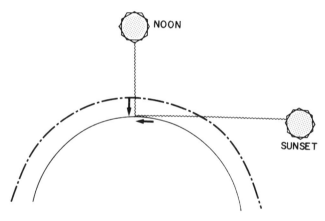

Illustration 84

The general appearance of the daytime sky, a blue field containing a yellow sun, can thus be understood in terms of the scattering of sunlight by the molecules that make up the atmosphere. But what of the dust and other particulate matter we know to be in the air? Do they have any observable effect?

When light encounters a large object, most of the energy of the incoming wave scatters into a small cone pointing forward instead of being scattered in all directions, and all colors are scattered equally. We would expect, then, that the effects of particulate matter in the air would not be to contribute to the blue sky effect. Instead particles take the light from the sun and scatter it as shown in Illustration 85. This scattering from particles must be added to that from molecules, just as the surf in our analogy is scattered both by the forest of needles and the large rocks. The net effect of these two kinds of scattering is shown in Illustration 86. An observer looking at the sky in directions away from the sun will see the ordinary blue light that results from molecular scattering. The presence or absence of particles will not affect this result. If the observer looks at the sky near the sun, however, he

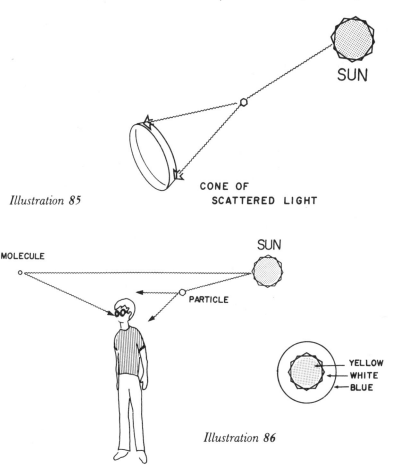

SUN

Illustration 85

CONE OF
SCATTERED LIGHT

MOLECULE

SUN

PARTICLE

YELLOW
WHITE
BLUE

Illustration 86

will see light that has been scattered from the incoming beam by particles in the air. Since these particles scatter all wavelengths equally, this cone of light will be white in color. The sky, then, will have the appearance shown on the right in Illustration 86. There will be blue sky far away from the sun, shading into a bright ring surrounding the sun.

One note of warning. NEVER look directly at the sun—even with dark glasses. Doing so can cause eye damage or even permanent blindness.

The presence of particles in the air, then, does contribute to the appearance of the sky near the sun. I have noticed that the bright area around the sun seems noticeably smaller when seen from high mountains in Montana, where I spend my summers. I have been told by those who have worked on scientific expeditions in the Antarctic, where the air is very clean, that the bright region is almost nonexistent there, and that the blue sky goes right up to the edge of the sun itself. Both of these facts are easily understood if we realize that the clear air of the Montana mountains (or of Antarctica) contains relatively few particles, so that almost all the scattered light comes from molecules.

But having explained the appearance of the sky by the way light is scattered in the atmosphere, it is a good idea to pause for a moment to recall one important fact. Most of the visible light from the sun that enters the atmosphere is not scattered at all, but comes right through. The atmosphere is a highly transparent medium, a fact each of us can verify from our own experience in viewing distant objects. For example, it is not at all uncommon in Montana to see the outlines of mountain ranges over a hundred miles away, but one does not have to travel to relatively unpopulated areas to confirm this phenomenon. From the balcony outside the theoretical physics offices at Berkeley, in California, one can, on a clear day, see the Farallon Islands, fifty miles out to sea. From these and similar experiences, we know that light can travel great distances through the atmosphere. We also know that at altitudes of 30,000 feet (six miles) the air is very thin, so we are led to the conclusion that it is possible for light to travel through the air for much longer distances than are required to bring sunlight down to the surface of the earth. Therefore, although the molecules in the atmosphere create the blue sky by scattering some of the sunlight that comes through, they are actually rather inefficient scattering centers.

In our analogy with the surf, therefore, the forest of needles that represented the atmospheric scattering centers should really be thought of as a forest of something much more porous. If you can imagine a one-eighth-inch needle made of an open weblike material, you have a pretty good notion of the power of an ordinary atom to scatter a light wave (or any kind of electromagnetic radiation) that impinges on it.

We have already touched on the reason for this inefficiency. When an electron is bound to an atom, it is difficult for the incoming wave to cause it to accelerate. The nucleus of the atom binds the electron too tightly to allow it to absorb and reemit much light. This suggests that if the electrons were freed from the nuclei (as they would be, for example, at very high temperatures) they would be much more efficient scatterers of light.

A medium in which atoms have been dissociated into electrons and nuclei is called a plasma. Plasmas are routinely created in our laboratories. They are also quite common in the universe. The high temperatures found in most stars (including the sun) guarantee that most of the material in them will be in the plasma state. Consequently, scientists have had ample opportunity to study the interaction of radiation with plasmas, and, as might be expected, they have found that radiation tends to be scattered much more from the free electrons than from electrons bound into atoms.

Perhaps the most interesting example of this scattering process occurs in our own sun. Radiation is generated in the core of the sun by nuclear fusion and begins streaming outward. It does not proceed in a straight line, as it might in the earth's atmosphere, but is scattered again and again by the plasma. In a vacuum, light would be able to travel from the sun's center to its surface, a distance of some 500,000 miles, in less than three seconds. The scattering in the plasma is so severe, however, and the actual zigzag path of the light so convoluted, that it actually takes a given bit of radiation about a million years to make the trip to the surface. The sunshine that is falling on you today actually began its outward journey at about the time that *Homo sapiens* appeared on the surface of the earth!

Just as pumping water into a container from which it cannot easily escape produces a high pressure, so too does the constant stream of radiation produced by the fusion reaction and released into the main body of the sun produce a force that tends to blow the sun apart. It is this force—the so-called radiation pressure—that counteracts gravity and keeps the sun from collapsing. The long-term stability of the sun results from the balancing of these two effects. A material in which light scatters very little is said to be transparent, because most of the light that hits it goes right through. The lack of transparency of the material in the sun is extremely important. If the sun were as transparent as the earth's atmosphere, the radiation generated at the core would escape, exerting very little pressure in the process. In this case, gravity would take over and the sun would collapse.

The transparency (or lack of it) in astronomical materials played a very important role in the early history of our universe. We theorize that our universe began in a Big Bang some 10 to 15 billion years ago, and that in its early stages it consisted of unimaginably dense and hot material. During the first tenth of a second or so, the temperatures were so high that neither atoms nor nuclei could exist. At that point, for example, the temperature was about 30 billion degrees (Centigrade), much hotter than the center of even the hottest star. It wasn't until the universe was three minutes old that the temperature fell to a billion degrees and it was possible for stable nuclei of hydrogen and helium to form and for matter to exist as plasma. The radiation created in the Big Bang and the nuclear processes that followed it created a pressure in this plasma, much as a radiation pressure is maintained in the sun. This pressure prevented the rapid collapse of the protouniverse under gravity and allowed the expansion to go on.

A mixture of sugar and water, initially cloudy, becomes transparent as the sugar dissolves. A similar process occurred early in the history of the universe. Photos by Judith Peatross.

And expand it did, for thousands of years. During this entire time, the cooling, expanding plasma remained opaque to radiation, and the radiation pressure prevented the formation of any clumps of matter like stars or galaxies. Even though electrons in the plasma might occasionally combine with a proton or helium nucleus to form an atom, the collisions between bits of matter were violent enough to guarantee that the electron would be knocked off before long.

An extremely important turning point was then reached. After the cooling process had gone on for about five hundred thousand years, the temperature dropped to the point where electrons could stay bound into atoms despite the collisions. The plasma disappeared, to be replaced by a collection of atoms not unlike the forest of needles in our surf analogy. The material of the universe became transparent to radiation, no radiation pressure existed to balance gravity, and the slow collapse of matter into galaxies, stars, and planets could begin. Were it not that it is difficult for radiation to accelerate a bound electron, the radiation pressure in the early universe might have remained high enough to prevent gravitational collapse. In this case, there might very well have been no galaxies formed at all.

Astrophysicists refer to the process by which electrons moved into atoms and the material of the universe became transparent as the decoupling of radiation from matter. There is an everyday experience that can give some insight into the decoupling process. If you mix some sugar in a glass of water, you will note that at first the mixture appears cloudy. The sugar turns the clear water translucent because, initially at least, the sugar is suspended in the water in the form of large grains. These grains are similar to the particulate matter in the atmosphere. They are fairly efficient scatterers of light, which means that light entering one side of the glass holding your mixture will not be able to get through without being scattered. This is the reason you get a diffused sort of illumination when you hold the glass up to a light bulb. You can think of the sugar-water mixture in this state as being somewhat analogous to the early universe. Both were filled with material that was efficient at scattering radiation, although, of course, the nature of the scattering material is very different in the two cases.

If you keep stirring the mixture, in a short time it will suddenly become transparent. If you hold it to a light, you will be able to see the lamp quite clearly. In fact, there will be virtually no detectable difference now, optically speaking, between the formerly translucent mixture and ordinary water. The cause of this transformation is quite simple. The large grains of sugar dissolve and enter the solution as individual molecules. As we now know, individual molecules are actually very poor scatterers; hence they are not able to affect the light passing through the mixture. The sudden clearing that we see, then, is a good analog to the sudden clearing of the universe when radiation and matter decoupled.

So, the next time you are sitting in a restaurant stirring the sugar into your iced tea, you might pause and reflect that what you are seeing happen in your glass is not so different from the process that made possible the formation of stars and planets out of the primordial matter resulting from the Big Bang.

12

The Grand
Unification

ONE OF THE LIGHTER MOMENTS IN THE APOLLO PROGRAM occurred when astronaut Alan Shepard took out a golf club and hit the first drive on the moon. To no one's surprise, the ball traveled much farther than it would have on earth. The reason for this, as we all know, is that things weigh less on the moon. To say it another way, the force of gravity is less on the moon than it is on earth.

But what, exactly, is gravity? Aristotle taught that everything was filled with a sort of motive force that impelled it to seek the center of the universe—a point that the Greeks identified with the center of the earth. By this sort of reasoning, a heavy object would have more motive force, and therefore would be expected to fall to earth more quickly, than a lighter one. According to the folklore, Galileo was the first to prove that this idea was wrong, by dropping weights from the leaning tower of Pisa. It's easy to show that

This television picture of the Apollo 14 mission on the moon shows astronaut Alan B. Shepard, Jr., preparing to swing at a golf ball. Shepard used an actual six iron attached to the end of the handle for the contingency sample return, and a real golf ball. Photo courtesy of the National Aeronautics and Space Administration.

he could never really have done this particular experiment. The force of wind resistance during the fall would have caused the heavier weight to hit the ground first, thereby confirming, rather than refuting, Aristotle's teachings. But by whatever means, Galileo did discover that the rate at which an object will fall, ignoring secondary effects like wind resistance, is the same for everything on the earth.

It remained for Isaac Newton to state the law of gravitation in its modern form. Whether he was inspired to do so by seeing an apple fall or whether the inspiration came from some other source, the result is one of the most far-reaching laws of modern science. It states that there is a force between any two massive objects in the universe that tends to pull them toward each other, a force we call gravity. The more massive the objects are and the closer they are together, the greater the force. In the mathematical language used by physicists, Newton's law for two masses m_1 and m_2 is usually stated as follows:

$$F = G \frac{m_1 m_2}{r^2}$$

In words, this formula says that F, the force of gravity between any two objects, can be calculated by the following steps: (1) multiply the masses of the two objects together, (2) divide by the square of the distance between them, and (3) multiply the result by a universal constant, G, known as the gravitational constant. In the system of units where mass is measured in kilograms and distances in meters, G has the numerical value 6.67×10^{-11}.

The first thing to notice about the force of gravity is that it is very small, since the constant G has ten zeros to the right of the decimal point before the first number appears. The second thing to notice is that the force of gravity acts between *any* two objects in the universe, no matter how small or how far apart. It is not something that is unique to large bodies like the earth.

For example, if you weigh 176 pounds your mass is 80 kilograms. This book might have a mass of half a kilogram. If you stand one meter (about three feet) from the book, there will be a force pulling you toward the book and a force pulling the book toward you. This is exactly the same sort of force that keeps you on the earth and prevents you from floating off into space. It is the force of gravity. You can't feel the gravitational attraction of the book because it is very small, corresponding to about one ten-billionth of a pound. It would take a high precision measuring instrument to measure a force that small, and our comparatively gross kinesthetic senses are just not up to the job.

The ubiquity of the gravitational force is sometimes used by astrologers to justify their assumption that the positions of the stars and the planets at the moment of birth can exert an influence on a person's life. The argument is that since the force of gravity is known to act no matter how far away the influencing body is, there should be no objection to saying that planets and nearby stars could have something to do with human destinies.

Like so many pseudoscientific arguments, this one seems plausible until you look at it closely. From Newton's law of gravity, it's clear that a star the size of the sun (2×10^{30} Kg) at a distance of five light years (3.8×10^{16} meters) away will exert a gravitational force on a newborn baby at the moment of birth. But so will everything else in the universe, including a 100-Kg doctor standing 1 meter away. In fact, if you use Newton's law to calculate the relative sizes of the forces exerted by the nearby doctor and by the faraway star you will find the following:

$$\frac{F_{doctor}}{F_{star}} = \frac{2.7 \times 10^{-8}}{3.7 \times 10^{-13}} \approx 10^5 = 100,000$$

In other words, just by shifting his weight from one foot to another during the delivery, the doctor can exert a gravitational force on the emerging baby that is 100,000 times as great as that exerted by the nearest star. So much for the use of Newton to "prove" astrology.

That the gravitational force is so small means that in order to produce a sizeable gravitational effect, large amounts of material must be gathered together. Anyone who has ever carried a heavy package up a flight of stairs knows that gravity is a force to be reckoned with on earth, and the reason for its importance in our daily lives is quite simple. We spend these lives located about four thousand miles from the center of a very large mass (the earth), and Newton's equation tells us that large masses will exert large forces. Since the moon is considerably less massive than the earth, the fact that a golf ball could be driven farther on the lunar surface also follows directly from Newton's law.

But there is an important aspect to this argument that is often overlooked in modern treatments of gravity. From a philosophical point of view, Newton's law is important not because it gives a precise formula for calculating forces, but because it was the first truly *universal* law of nature that the human race discovered.

When we talk about hitting a golf ball on the moon, we make an assumption that seems so obvious to us we are scarcely aware of it. We assume that the law of gravity operating here on the earth also operates on the moon—that gravity is the same everywhere. Yet until a few hundred years ago—for most of the intellectual history of the human race—this assumption would have been rejected out of hand. To the great Greek philosophers, the heavens were ruled by the laws of geometry, laws accessible to pure reason, while earthly things, made of corruptible matter, behaved quite differently. This preoccupation with the perfection of the heavens is best illustrated by their insistence that the planets moved in perfect circles through the turning of celestial spheres. To them, the idea that the force that makes an apple fall and the force that holds the moon in its orbit are the same would have seemed ludicrous.

The details of the way that Newton actually came to the conclusion that this might be the case is not important. For our purposes, it is enough to notice that he felt he had verified his law when he calculated the moon's orbit and found it to agree (within a rather large experimental uncertainty) with what was observed. By bringing the earthly and the heavenly together in this way, Newton produced the first great unification in the history of science. Two areas that had seemed diverse were now seen to be governed by a single law, and an artificial distinction in the minds of human beings had been erased.

It was well over a century after Newton that the next great unification in physics began to emerge. The new unification brought together two phenomena that are clearly different from each other—electricity and magnetism. Both these phenomena had been known for a long time. The Greeks were well aware that the rocks they called lodestones could attract bits of metal. There was even a legend that somewhere in the Mediterranean there was an island made completely of this material, and that a ship unlucky enough to approach it would have all the nails in its structure pulled out. In medieval times the Chinese built a useable compass based on the fact that a needle-shaped lodestone will always point toward the North Pole, an idea that was greatly elaborated upon by European navigators before and during the age of exploration. So, by the beginning of the nineteenth century, a good deal of empirical knowledge had been gained about the behavior of magnets.

The development of the science of electricity was somewhat slower, primarily because there was no practical application like the compass to encourage it. The Greeks knew that certain materials, like glass and amber, acquired the ability, when rubbed, to pick up small bits of material. If you comb your own hair on a dry day and then bring the comb near some bits of paper, you will see the same thing. This phenomenon, which we now call static electricity, did not become a subject of major scientific research until well into the eighteenth century. The "electricians" of that century were primarily motivated by scientific curiosity in their studies. It was the discovery of the electrical nature of lightning by Benjamin Franklin that led to the first practical electrical device, the lightning rod. But by the end of the century, the practical aspects of lightning protection, coupled with the development of devices like the storage battery, had brought the knowledge of electricity to where it could be said to be as well understood as magnetism was at the time.

The important thing about this situation is not the details of what was known in those two areas of study, but that there is absolutely no reason to suspect they should be related in any way. After all, what does the behavior of a piece of magnetized iron in a compass have to do with bits of paper sticking to a comb? The phenomena associated with the two disciplines seem so disparate that only the advantage of hindsight causes us to discuss them in the same chapter. Nevertheless, a series of experimental and theoretical discoveries that spanned the middle years of the nineteenth century showed that electricity and magnetism are not only related to each other, but can be thought of as being nothing more than different aspects of the same fundamental process in nature.

The discovery that typifies this unification was made in 1820 by the Danish physicist Hans Christian Oersted. He discovered that if a wire is connected across a battery so that electrical charges flow in it, a compass that is brought near the wire will be deflected. The compass will behave just as if it had been brought near a large magnet. This discovery is the basis for the electromagnet discussed in chapter 6, but it has a deep philosophical significance as well. It shows that there is a fundamental connection between electrical and magnetic phenomena—a connection unknown before Oersted's discovery. Other such connections were discovered. For example, it was found that a magnet moved around near a loop of wire would cause electrical currents to flow in the wire. In a similar vein, it was discovered that a changing electrical field could produce magnetic effects. Far from being separate and distinct disciplines, electricity and magnetism were becoming more and more intertwined.

This unity was given its fullest statement in 1865, when the Scottish physicist James Clerk Maxwell published what are known today as Maxwell's equations. These equations summarized all that is known about both electricity and magnetism and established once and for all that it is impossible to describe one without bringing in the other. It's hard to think of a more convincing proof that the two effects are, in fact, aspects of a single natural phenomenon.

Just as Newton's original unification of gravity led to the development of a number of practical applications, such as the theory of the tides, the electromagnetic unification was not slow in producing important results. For example, Maxwell was able to show that his equation implied the existence of waves with electrical and magnetic properties that would travel through free space at the speed of light, but that would have different wavelengths, depending on the nature of the electrical disturbance creating them. These are now called radio waves, and their discovery and exploitation in the late nineteenth century began the modern communication revolution. So, although the idea of unification in nature is profoundly important in a philosophical sense, it has also always produced practical results in the past.

The success of these sorts of unification led scientists to wonder if a further unification between gravity and electricity might not be found. Throughout the latter part of the nineteenth century, many brilliant people spent a lot of time trying to produce theories in which gravity and electromagnetism were taken to be different aspects of a single force, much as Maxwell's theory takes electricity and magnetism to be. Such theories, should they be found, are usually called unified theories, or perhaps unified field theories, since we commonly speak of both electromagnetic and gravitational fields. In the nineteenth century, the attempt to unify gravity with electromagnetism produced theories based on Newton's laws of mechanical motion. In this century, both Albert Einstein and Werner Heisenberg (one of the founders of modern quantum theory) spent the latter parts of their lives trying to find different ways to unify. But for most of the twentieth century, this particular quest was well outside the mainstream of scientific thought. One reason was that scientists, preoccupied with sorting out the newly discovered world of the atom and the nucleus, had no time to devote to the problem. Another reason is that as we learned more about the atom and its nucleus, it became obvious that there were forces in the world that hadn't been dreamed of by the classical physicist.

The new forces are termed the strong and the weak forces, and they play their most important roles in the realm of the atomic nucleus and the particles within it. The strong force can be thought of as a sort of glue that holds protons and neutrons together in the nucleus—an object about 10^{-13} cm across. The term *strong* is used because this force must overcome the enormous repulsive electrical forces that exist between positively charged particles like the protons when they are forced so close together. The weak force, on the other hand, governs the radioactive decay of some unstable nuclei and particles. The term *weak* is applied because the decay can sometimes take a very long time to happen, a fact that physicists took to be an indication that the force driving the decay could not be very powerful.

Once these two forces were added to the roster, the outlook for unification seemed quite dim. Not only did their presence double the number of forces that needed to be unified, but the forces are so different from each other that at first glance it seemed to be impossible that they could ever be unified in the same way as electricity and magnetism. The fact that a person of Einstein's capabilities could spend thirty years in a fruitless search for a unified field theory was taken as strong evidence that such a theory simply didn't exist, and that nature had to be explained in terms of four fundamental, but distinct, forces.

The differences between these forces are truly awesome. Gravity and electromagnetism, for example, can act over very long distances as shown by our example of the gravitational attraction of a nearby star. The strong and weak forces, however, act over distances almost a hundred thousand times smaller than the size of an atom. How can it be possible to think of two forces as being one and the same if one is found acting only over a small distance and the others over any distance?

Another important difference is the relative strength of these forces. As the name implies, the strong interaction, even though it operates only over distances comparable to the size of a nucleus, is capable of producing the greatest effects. The hierarchy of strength then descends through the electromagnetic, weak, and gravitational forces. The strengths of the four fundamental interactions relative to the strong force are given in the following table.

Force	Relative strength
strong	1
electromagnetic	$1/137$
weak	10^{-5}
gravitational	6×10^{-39}

Last, and perhaps most important, the theories that have been proposed to explain each of the four forces are very different. In chapter 2 we said that general relativity, the theory underlying our modern ideas about gravitation, comes from considerations that are essentially geometrical. By contrast, the modern theories for the other three forces deal with a microscopic process called particle exchange. In this way of looking at things, the force between two given particles results from the exchange of a third particle. In pictorial terms, the two particles move along as shown in Illustration 87, and then, at some point in time, the third par-

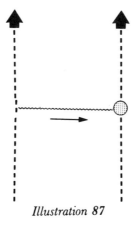

Illustration 87

ticle is emitted by one and absorbed by the other. The net effect of the exchange is that a force—either attractive or repulsive—is generated.

The idea of a force being due to an exchanged particle comes out of modern theory and is somewhat difficult to visualize. Perhaps the following analogy will help. Think of two ice skaters approaching each other in such a way that they will pass at some distance from each other. When the skaters are near each other, one throws a snowball at the other. The recoil from the act of throwing will cause the first skater's direction of motion to change as shown in Illustration 88. Similarly, the second skater will recoil in the opposite direction when she catches (or is hit by) the snowball. The overall effect of throwing the snowball, then, is to cause the paths of the two skaters to be deflected, *exactly as if they had collided with one another.* Since we would agree that in the event of a collision the two skaters would have exerted forces on each other, we come to the conclusion that the exchange of the snowball produces the same effect as a force.

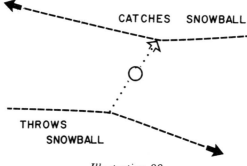

CATCHES SNOWBALL

THROWS
SNOWBALL

Illustration 88

In theories that involve exchanged particles, the differences between the interactions have to do with the differences between the particles that are exchanged to create the force. In general, the heavier the exchanged particle the shorter the distance it can travel. Short-range forces will be associated with the exchange of heavy particles, while long-range forces will be associated with the exchange of light particles. We think of electromagnetism as being associated with the exchange of a particle called the photon. This is the same particle that constitutes light, radio waves, and X-rays. It has zero rest mass, and hence the force has a very long range. (The concept of zero mass seems a little strange at first. For our purposes, think of a zero-mass particle as something that can exert a force when it collides with another particle but wouldn't weigh anything if you put it on a scale.)

The strong force is associated with the exchange of particles roughly as massive as the proton and neutron, and has a range of 10^{-13} cm—about the size of the atomic nucleus. The weak force is associated with the exchange of a particle whose existence has been predicted, but which has yet to be seen in the laboratory. This particle goes by the name of the heavy vector boson and has a mass roughly 100 times that of the proton. Consequently, the range of the weak force is only about 10^{-15} cm, considerably smaller than the size of the nucleus. Illustration 89 is a diagrammatic picture of each of these three forces in terms of particle exchange diagrams.

The essential point about these three forces is this: In each case, we explain what we know about the forces in terms of the behavior of elementary particles. This necessarily involves the use of quantum mechanics, the science that governs the atomic and subatomic world. *Every* quantum mechanical description of a force must involve a diagram like those in Illustration 89. That we

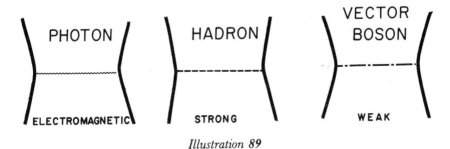

Illustration 89

have not included a diagram for the fourth force—gravity—does not mean that gravity is necessarily fundamentally different in this regard. It simply means that we do not yet possess a theory of gravitation that includes quantum mechanics. We do not really know how to deal with gravity on the atomic scale, and, consequently, we do not really know how to describe gravity in the same way as we explain the other three forces. Physicists have suggested that someday we will be able to explain gravity in terms of the exchange of a zero-mass particle called the graviton, but bringing our knowledge of gravity into line with our knowledge of the other forces remains one of the major unsolved problems in modern physics.

The fundamental difference between general relativity (gravitation) and the other forces may explain why Einstein failed in his attempt to unify all the forces into a single, relativitylike theory. It may be that it's just the hardest way to go about uniting the forces. The most important evidence for this particular conjecture is that during the last decade enormous progress has been made in the quest for a unified theory, but this progress has come about through work on the three other forces, with gravity still excluded so far.

In 1979 Abdus Salam, Sheldon Glashow, and Steven Weinberg shared the Nobel Prize in physics for taking the first step in the move toward unification since Maxwell. They showed that it was possible to have a theory in which the weak and electromagnetic interactions are, at some fundamental level, the same. In view of what we have said about the apparent disparity between these two, what are we to make of this development?

Perhaps an analogy will help. Think of a crystal such as ordinary rock salt. A crystal has a definite shape, as shown in Illustration 90. The flat planes of the crystal's sides define directions in space, and the direction we have labeled UP is quite different from the one we have labeled SIDEWAYS. It would appear impossible to provide an explanation of the crystal structure with a theory in which UP and SIDEWAYS were not distinguishable.

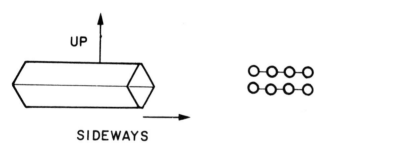

Illustration 90

But suppose we look at the crystal more closely. If we look with a microscope capable of seeing small groups of atoms, we'd see something like the middle figure in Illustration 90. Although we no longer have clean planes, the enlarged picture still shows the atoms arrayed in specific directions in space, and UP and SIDEWAYS are still different.

Now let's increase the power of our microscope until we look closely at a single atom in the crystal. The single atom could very well be the featureless sphere shown on the right in Illustration 90. For this sphere, there is no preferred direction. The atom is the same whether we look at it in the UP direction or in the SIDEWAYS direction. In other words, it is possible to describe a crystal that has a clear orientation in space in terms of atoms for which all directions are identical. All we have to do to see the underlying symmetry of the seemingly asymmetrical crystal is look with a large enough magnification.

The idea of the unification of the electromagnetic and weak interactions is the same. The two look very different to us, just as UP and SIDEWAYS appear to be different in the crystal. But just as the crystal revealed an underlying symmetry when we looked at it closely enough, so too do we expect the seemingly different forces to display their similarity when we have enough magnification. This is the approach taken in the so-called Weinberg-Salam theory. We have pointed out the connection between the mass of the exchanged particle and the range of the force with which it is associated. Since mass and energy are related, it should not be too surprising to learn that increasing the magnifying power of the "microscope" we use to examine elementary particles corresponds to using higher and higher energy probes. According to the theory, the weak and electromagnetic interactions should start to look identical when the probe energies get to about one hundred times the mass of the proton. At this energy level (which will be available in a few large accelerator laboratories), we expect to "see" that the electromagnetic and weak interactions are identical, just as the crystal revealed an underlying identity between UP and SIDEWAYS in our previous example when we examined it on a small enough scale.

The Weinberg-Salam theory makes some predictions about the results of experiments on large accelerators, and many of these predictions were checked in the laboratory in the mid-1970s. The predictions were verified in all cases, and the theory is now accepted by most physicists. With this theory, the number of fundamental forces in nature is reduced from four to three. We now have only gravity and strong and "electroweak" interactions.

The success of the electroweak unification leads to an obvious question. If increasing the magnification of our microscope to one level reveals the basic identity of two seemingly dissimilar interactions, will increasing the magnification still further show that the strong interaction is also identical? In other words, is it possible that there is some energy at which the strong, weak, and electromagnetic forces will all be unified?

The quest for a theory that unifies all three of these forces is going ahead full tilt in physics today. It turns out that the energy needed to "see" the three forces as being identical is about 10^{15} times the mass of the proton—an energy that will be impossible to achieve in a machine in the foreseeable future. Nonetheless, the authors of the so-called grand unification theories (GUT) have been able to produce some predictions that can be checked against experiment. The most interesting of these concern the stability of the proton. In the conventional wisdom, the proton is absolutely stable. It does not decay, and every proton that was around after the Big Bang is still here somewhere.

If the strong and electroweak interactions are really the same, however, there must be a minute probability that a proton left to itself can spontaneously decay into other kinds of particles. Such processes occur all the time for other particles, but they have never been observed for the proton. If it should turn out that the proton is not absolutely stable, as was previously thought, the way that the new-found instability can be measured is to speak of the proton lifetime. This is the time it would take a given proton to decay. The longer this time is, the more stable the proton will appear.

As of this writing, it is known that the lifetime of the proton must be at least 10^{30} years, a number that is huge compared to the 10^{10} years since the Big Bang. The GUT, however, predicts that the proton lifetime should be about 10^{31} years—tantalizingly close to the present experimental limit. Sometime soon, the results of a new round of experiments on proton lifetimes should become known. If it is found that the proton does indeed decay (albeit rarely), it will be a tremendous boost for the unification theories.

As you read this, the quest for unification has become one of the main areas of endeavor in modern physics. Three of the four fundamental forces have been unified. We are left with only two basic interactions in nature: the strong-electroweak and gravity. And who can tell? Perhaps even gravity will be added to the fold in our lifetimes, and the old dream of explaining all of nature in terms of a single force will be realized.

Index